PRAISE FOR

GOD'S BOLD CALL TO WOMEN

God's Bold Call to Women is a cutting-edge voice to men and women around the world. Women are changing nations, and this book will give them the strength they need to follow the call of God.

CINDY JACOBS
Cofounder, Generals of Intercession
Author, *The Supernatural Life* and *The Voice of God*

Barbara Yoder's masterful writing ability is evident as she challenges women to arise into their God-given calling. I consider this book a must-read for all who seek to understand God's unique plan for women.

BARBARA WENTROBLE
Founder, International Breakthrough Ministries
Author, *Prophetic Intercession, You Are Anointed* and
God's Purpose for Your Life

GOD'S BOLD CALL TO WOMEN

BARBARA J. YODER
GENERAL EDITOR

Regal

From Gospel Light
Ventura, California, U.S.A.

PUBLISHED BY REGAL BOOKS
FROM GOSPEL LIGHT
VENTURA, CALIFORNIA, U.S.A.
PRINTED IN THE U.S.A.

Regal Books is a ministry of Gospel Light, a Christian publisher dedicated to serving the local church. We believe God's vision for Gospel Light is to provide church leaders with biblical, user-friendly materials that will help them evangelize, disciple and minister to children, youth and families.

It is our prayer that this Regal book will help you discover biblical truth for your own life and help you meet the needs of others. May God richly bless you.

For a free catalog of resources from Regal Books/Gospel Light, please call your Christian supplier or contact us at 1-800-4-GOSPEL *or* www.regalbooks.com.

Originally published as *Mantled with Authority: God's Apostolic Call to Women* by Wagner Publications in 2003.
Regal Books edition published in May 2005.
© 2003 Barbara J. Yoder
All rights reserved.

Library of Congress Cataloging-in-Publication Data
Mantled with authority.
   God's bold call to women / [edited by] Barbara J. Yoder.
      p. cm.
   Originally published: Mantled with authority. Colorado Springs, Colo.: Wagner Publications, 2003.
   Includes bibliographical references (p.   ) and index.
   ISBN 0-8307-3719-7 (trade pbk.)
   1. Women in Christianity. 2. Women clergy. 3. Church—Apostolicity. I. Yoder, Barbara J. II. Title.
   BV639.W7M294 2005
   262'.14'082—dc22   2005002514

2   3   4   5   6   7   8   9   10   /   10   09   08   07   06   05

Rights for publishing this book in other languages are contracted by Gospel Light Worldwide, the international nonprofit ministry of Gospel Light. Gospel Light Worldwide also provides publishing and technical assistance to international publishers dedicated to producing Sunday School and Vacation Bible School curricula and books in the languages of the world. For additional information, visit www.gospellightworldwide.org; write to Gospel Light Worldwide, P.O. Box 3875, Ventura, CA 93006; or send an e-mail to info@gospellightworldwide.org.

DEDICATION

To my parents, Burton H. Jones and Ruth H. Jones, for building a foundation of biblical character and integrity in my life. My father lived a life of integrity and character and taught me to follow in his steps. My mother taught me to learn the Word of God and to talk to God. She taught me about social justice. To my step-mother, Marie, who found her seed of destiny and has stood by my father's side for 35 years with faithfulness and joy.

To my spiritual mothers (mentors) in the Lord, who imparted to me a passion for the Word, prayer, knowing God and integrity of life as well as loved me unconditionally. They helped to make me who and what I am today. I salute them:

Myrtle D. Beall, pastor of Bethesda Missionary Temple in Detroit, Michigan, who has already gone on to be with the Lord.

Her daughter Patricia Beall Gruits, founder and director of Rhema International (Rochester, Michigan), a missions organization to Haiti. She laid a powerful foundation in my life and continues to this day to be a wonderful "mother," encourager and friend—a great woman in God who continues to follow God with passion.

Wanda Gehring, "an ordinary homemaker and wife," who helped me find the way out of my past and move with freedom into my future in God. She is one of God's secret weapons who, though hidden behind the frontlines, powerfully influenced my life at a critical time.

CONTENTS

INTRODUCTION

Woman, this is the day for which you were born—for such a time as this. It is a day of freedom, a day of boldness, when we can come out of a place of hiding and begin to connect with our apostolic mandate. This book is written to motivate and encourage women to move into the place of significance to which God has called us. This is a day in which the whole Church is being freed and is arising to take its rightful place. As you read this book, let it both heal and empower you for this new day.

How did this book come about? I recognized people were addressing women's issues through books and conferences. They either spoke on how to be a better woman or laid out an apologetic explaining why women could do anything in addition to being a wife or a mother. Many great books have been published on the subject, and I have listed some in the Suggested Reading section; however, I found nothing written to specifically motivate women to break through into their apostolic mandate. I chose to hold a conference addressing the apostolic call on women. From that conference, it became clear that the Body of Christ would benefit greatly from a book written directly addressing the topic, and that a collaborative effort would offer a well-rounded point of view.

I knew it was imperative to invite authors who had national authority or represented different aspects of the issue; therefore, I asked the following people to contribute a chapter to this book.

First, I invited **Chuck Pierce**. In Judges 4 and 5, Deborah was the apostolic, national leader. She had a general, named Barak, work with her so that the enemy of Israel could be overcome. Men and women coming into partnership is key for this next level of breakthrough. Chuck is a Barak who clearly understands the spirit behind the oppression of women. He is a national and international leader with apostolic authority in the nation. God has called him to come alongside women at strategic times and help propel them into their place. He is a strategist who can see the path ahead and has a good understanding of the unique gifts women have, as well as some of the snares they may face. In his chapter, Chuck explains these snares as well as the strategies needed to maneuver them, so that women can apprehend their destiny.

Apostle Wanda Studdard, with her husband, Apostle G. E. Studdard, are African American leaders who are breaking through in a city that has been challenging and even oppositional to African Americans. Wanda Studdard is bold and pioneering. When she hears from God, nothing can hold her back. She is a great woman who has an awesome heart for God, people, cities and the nation, and she is truly modeling the apostolic role for women. I have been in relationship with both Wanda and her husband for several years and esteem them highly. Apostle Studdard speaks with authority, both as a woman and a member of a minority group, directly addressing these two areas of oppression.

Jean Hodges is a beautiful, stately woman who has always stood at her husband's side. Her husband, Jim, leads a large, apostolic network. The first time I saw Jean, I thought a queen had just walked into the room. She is the model of a good wife and mother. Yet there has been a call within her, crying out to be heard. She ignored it for years, but there came a day when she could no longer disregard it. Jean has a call that is powerful and penetrating. She did not start walking in this call until she was 60. What a testimony to the power of the seed. Now Jean is traveling and speaking in this nation as well as others. She is impacting the world with a Deborah/Esther call. I asked her to write a chapter for those women who think they are now too old to fulfill the call of God or feel they have missed their window of opportunity.

Jane Hansen has unique authority in that she is the international CEO of Women's Aglow, and also a woman apostle—an Esther who has been called for such a time as this. She is a wonderful, gracious woman who leads courageously with feminine grace. She understands that women must walk not as anarchists, but boldly and as co-laborers with men in a way that will release the harvest. She is a beautiful woman, called for this day. She stands with international authority as well as authority in the issue we are dealing with in this book. No one understands the call on women as Jane does.

We begin this book with Chuck Pierce explaining how women can get snared, yet still have God's wonderful restoration available to them. No matter where you have been, what snare has bruised your walk with God or in what offense you have been captured, you can move out of that place, arise, and step into a place of redemption. Rahab was caught in prostitution but moved out of it to help Joshua's men. As a result, her decision to change saved her and her whole family. Esther, an orphan, hesitated but then grabbed hold of Mordecai's challenge and saved a nation. Deborah not only brought a nation into victory, but also saved a whole generation.

No matter where you have been, there is a mandate, a seed, a mantle and the power of God present to break you through to the next place. This book is written to encourage you to grab hold of your future and let loose of your past. As you read this book, expect God to apprehend you to release His Kingdom on Earth in a totally new way.

CHAPTER I

REDEEMING WOMEN:

When Good Girls Go Bad, There Is a Plan
Chuck D. Pierce

In 1999, God visited me. As I awakened one morning, it was as if He dropped a blackboard in front of me with 10 subjects written on it. The subjects included anti-Semitism, lawlessness, militant Islam, the transference of wealth and women arising. I asked the Lord, "What are You showing me here?" By His Spirit He replied, "This is the future war of the Church." Rebecca Sytsema and I then wrote a book with this same title that has helped the Body of Christ understand the times in which we are living.[1] Within that book, we shared the relationship between the oppression of women and the anti-christ system. We shared how women would arise, empowered by God, to display the victory of His Kingdom in the earth realm. The book you now hold in your hands is another important step toward understanding God's redemptive plan for women. Redemption means to buy back or to pay the fine of someone who has been in prison. As we begin to think about God's apostolic call to women today, let's start by reviewing how women deviated from God's purpose of creation and then look at God's redemptive plan.

MISPLACED DESIRE

Just as the Lord said in Genesis 3 when He promised redemption to the human race after their fall in the Garden, we are about to see a reality of Genesis 3:15, "And I will put enmity between you and the woman, and between your seed and her Seed; He shall bruise your head, and you shall bruise His heel." In the account of the woman in the Garden, we see that her role was marred. In Genesis 3:6 her desire shifted from God to human wisdom. And then in Genesis 3:16 God says to the woman, "I will greatly multiply your sorrow and your conception; in pain you shall bring forth children; your desire shall be for your husband and he shall rule over you." This means that her desire has now shifted toward her husband. It was a misplaced desire that would allow domination to occur in her life. This did not diminish womanhood or giftedness, but it meant that there would have to be a different alignment to bring her back into the full redemptive role that God had originally planned for her.

In both the Old and New Testaments, numerous references provide multifaceted psychological insights into the word *desire*. In the Old Testament, *desire* meant much more than merely to long for, to ask for, or to demand. In Hebraic psychology the whole personality was involved in desire. Hence, desire could easily become covetousness, leading to envy and jealousy. Among the Hebrews, desire was the inclination of the soul or self. And when the whole soul lay behind an inclination or desire that was sinful, then the soul, it was said, "lusted a lust" (see Num. 11:4,6). It was against this kind of covetousness that the tenth commandment was directed (see Exod. 20:17), because when such sinful desire was given free rein, the well-being of the whole community was endangered (see Jer. 6:13-15). However, when desire is linked into the heart of God, it can have powerful results. Therefore, desire, being a function of the soul and an integral part of the emotion, can either lead women astray to the devices of the enemy or into the ultimate purpose of God.

"With the Apostolic Church rising and the apostolic gift being restored in the Body of Christ to produce a new order, the question of how women fit into God's plan for the days ahead is key."[2] Today we must ask how women will arise and influence the Kingdom and how we will see Satan's plan manifested on Earth through the oppression of women. These two parallel issues will be one of the ways we determine the progress of the Church in the future.

THE UNTAPPED RESOURCE OF WOMEN

The enemy either wants to oppress and stop women from becoming all that God has created them to be, or else he wants to enchain and enslave them to accomplish his will on Earth. Even though the enemy wants to oppress and seduce women, we are about to see women arise and influence the world in a way they have never done before! Undoubtedly, women are one of our most untapped resources.

David Yonggi Cho, Senior Pastor of the 700,000-plus member Yoido Full Gospel Church in Seoul, Korea, states that "for 5,000 years in Korea, women had no voice at all. They were only to cater to the needs of men. Then Christianity came and set women free. Especially in the church, women are free. In ministry, they are equal to men. They are licensed, they are ordained, they become deacons and elders, and they become cell leaders." While some argue that women should be silent in the church, Cho says that "once women are called into ministry, they no longer belong to the category of women. They are messengers of the Lord."[3]

I am excited about what God has done in women. I believe there are certain wars that will only be won by women. Women must be a part of this next move of God if we are to see the Body of Christ advance into harvest. In an article in *SpiritLed Woman*, Judy Jacobs, examining how "the kingdom of heaven suffers violence, and the violent take it by force" (Matt. 11:12), states "'The violent take it by force' means that an energetic force takes for itself what is rightfully its own. This is a season where violence is required to get things accomplished in the supernatural that could never be done in the natural. This requires a new level of courage, determination, perseverance and unwavering faith. Women who have never felt violent, will now arise in faith and believe God for the impossible."[4] We are about to see faith-filled women arise and change the course of the earth.

THE SNARES OVER WOMEN

There is no doubt God is using women in a great way. Because of this, we need to know that the enemy has a plan to use women in the wrong way. Therefore, we need to see the female gender fully liberated by the Spirit of the Lord. We need to ask the Lord what is it we must learn as we enter into this movement. In so doing, we need to consider the snares of the devil over women. We need to understand why good girls go bad, and realize that even when they go bad, God has a plan for them. I believe if we focus on this issue correctly, we can break the reproach that has been set against women. Further, we need to understand the alignment the female gender has made with the enemy and break its power of agreement. If we do this, we will see true liberation come to women. As I list these snares, please note that I am not saying that all individual women fall into all snares. However, these are traps that the enemy has been successful in using against the female gender in general.

Snare #1: Satan convinces her that God, or someone who represents authority in her life, is not giving her all she deserves.

When we read Genesis 3, we find the first confrontation that Woman (Eve) has with the enemy of God, Satan. However, she is not fully aware that this creature is also her enemy. When the Serpent confronts her with, "Has God indeed said, 'You shall not eat of every tree of the garden?'" (v. 1) she responds, "We may eat the fruit of the trees of the garden; but of the fruit of the tree which is in the midst of the garden, God has said, 'You shall not eat it, nor shall you touch it, lest you die'" (vv. 2-3) The Serpent then negates the authority of the voice and directive of God by saying, "You will not surely die. For God knows that in the day you eat of it your eyes will be opened, and you will be like God" (vv. 4-5). Notice how the desire of Eve shifted. Instead of desiring to obey and adhere to the boundaries and fruitfulness that God had promised, she was convinced by the enemy that in regard to her redemptive plan, the Lord was holding out on her and not allowing her to have something that should be available to her.

Snare #2: She chooses not to listen to God and revere Him, but to agree with the enemy.

Be careful not to come into agreement with the enemy regarding something on which God has already given you specific instruction. When the enemy speaks contrary to the voice of God, do not listen. We need to ask, *what made Eve agree with the enemy?* She agreed with another voice rather than with the voice of God that was instructing her to live in a way that released life, not death. Why? Satan offered her something she couldn't have. We must be very aware of not trying to get something out of God's time. Nor should we try and get something that God hasn't offered us. Jesus redeemed this issue with women when the devil tried to give Him all the worlds, nations and kingdoms of the world. Jesus knew He was already going to get everything the devil was offering Him. Therefore, He chose to wait for the Lord to hand it over to Him.

Snare #3: She believes the lie that women have been cursed by God; therefore, when the accuser comes, she agrees with him.

Notice that God did release a curse. But it was not over Woman alone. He first cursed the Serpent. A great deal of false teaching has declared that all of the earth's problems are Woman's fault. When God was in the Garden, trying to find Man and Woman to have communion with them, Man (Adam) said, "I heard Your voice in the garden, and I was afraid because I was naked; and I hid myself" (v. 10). God said, "Who told you that you were naked? Have you eaten from the tree of which I commanded you that you should not eat?" (v. 11). Adam replied, "The woman you gave to be with me, she gave me of the tree, and I ate" (v. 12) Notice what Man did. He turned and loosed the accuser of the brethren on women. Immediately, when Woman was deceived, the door to the accuser of the brethren was opened against her. This set a precedent of the accuser of the brethren against women. What I admire in Eve is how she responded: "The serpent deceived me, and I ate" (v. 13). Woman started a redemptive plan by telling the truth. So be truthful. Then look at what God began to do. He said to the Serpent, "Because you have done this, you are cursed" (v. 14). He then placed enmity for the Serpent in Woman's DNA.

Any time you listen to the voice of the enemy, there is a way out. Don't ever let the devil tell you there is no way out once you have been deceived. The only thing that will hold you in deception is pride. Eve did not stay in deception very long. She immediately came out by humbling herself and telling the truth.

Snare #4: She fails to manage her desires.

Desire entered Woman through her eyes. She saw that the fruit of the tree was desirable. God said Woman's desire would now be for her husband and he would rule over her. Suddenly, the desires of Woman became the thing she would have to battle with. Desire is a function of emotion. For God to single this out from the beginning means we must understand desire. In addition to what I have pointed out above, we need to understand that desire is linked to the heart and eyes. If a woman does not allow her emotions to be made whole in the Lord (what God desires for her), they will be shifted toward something other than God. Desire is that place where the enemy will come and test a woman over and over again, particularly when she starts moving forward spiritually. She will have to guard her emotions and desires very carefully. She must have the same desire God does in order to move into the fullness of God's plan for her life. This is very important.

Snare #5: She has a tendency to look back versus keeping her vision focused forward.

In Genesis 19 we find the story of Lot's wife. In the story, the angels tell Lot to escape for his life and to not look behind or stay anywhere on the plain. "Escape to the mountain lest you be destroyed" (Gen. 19:17). But his wife looked back.

Women seem to have a difficulty in letting go of the past and just saying, "I'm going to cut my losses and move on." Why? Because of the emotional ties many women have. As a precedent, Lot's wife had a future before her, but there was one condition for the future: don't look back. Some women are constantly looking back at the hard places in their lives where God has already said, "I'm calling you out of a place into a new place; you better move and move quickly since there is a window of opportunity." Other women are continually looking back at old wounds. This is not an hour to look back. So quit looking back at past failures and old wounds. For when you keep looking back, you lose your focus on coming into the next victory. Women, take your opportunity to move forward. Don't keep looking back at all the past hurts you've had. Let God deal with it and judge it, and you will move into the best that is yet ahead.

Snare #6: She has a tendency to not acknowledge God-given authority because of prejudice.

In Numbers 12 we find this principle. Miriam was one of the first prophetesses we see in the Bible, and she was a tremendous prophetess of God. She had an incredible gift of celebration and song. The Israelites had come out of Egypt, and I can just see her encouraging Moses along the way. She is right there with him. When he sings the song of the Lord, she begins to beat that tumbrel and sing with him—you can just imagine the Spirit of God.

But as they move forward and Moses comes to a place of leadership where he has to make decisions to corporately advance the entire nation, notice what she then does: "Miriam and Aaron spoke against Moses because of the Ethiopian woman whom he married" (Num 12:1). In other words, Miriam had a racial issue; and because she had this racial, sectarian issue, she opened her mouth and declared how she felt about Moses' wife. This had nothing to do with his ability as a leader—she just found an issue to target. And in that issue of racism, she caused the whole movement of God to stop. That's how simple it is.

In the next move of God, I believe women will be the agents to tear down racism in the earth. Protect yourself from the enemy who will target you to stir up racism. God loved Miriam so much that He did not want to proceed without her (see Num. 12:15). Similarly, He does not want to proceed in this time of history without the female gender being unified.

Snare #7: She allows the enemy to use her to seduce others out of God's perfect covenant plan.

We have a record in the book of Judges of two interesting women. One is Deborah, who led God's people into victory (see

Judg. 4). The other is Delilah. Delilah was an interesting cookie. She was a beautiful, gifted and influential woman who had things happening with her for good. However, she also had a way of manipulation. She actually had a hidden agenda to trap Samson (see Judg. 16).

This is going to be a season when God purifies women. When we enter a new apostolic dimension, God does a purifying work in us personally and corporately. So, at this time in history, do not allow hidden agendas and manipulation to trap you. If you do, you will allow the enemy to use you to seduce others and you will be harmed. Let God begin to purify and bring all of that out of you, for He is ready to use you. If you have hidden agendas, the enemy will find a way to trap you.

Snare #8. She has desire for power.

Jezebel is an important figure in biblical history as well as our prophetic future. In the book of 1 Kings, we find this woman controlling the whole nation (see 1 Kings 18). So, what is the snare for women? Jezebel was a worshiper of evil idols who controlled the entire government and atmosphere of a region. Because she worshiped wrongly, she began to be empowered by demons. She became so empowered by demons that she began to mobilize a false form of worship that affected an entire generation.

Please note that Jezebel is not someone in your church who tries to make sure everything is right all the time. This is a problem resulting from manipulation and control, and if this is the issue, you can break its power. Nor was Jezebel the woman always telling the pastor what to do. If we are moving into an apostolic season, women will have authority in the church. The issue here was that Jezebel was linked into sorcery and an evil worship system. She became the most influential person in the entire nation. She was filled with a covetous and murderous spirit. If there was something she desired in order to propel the evil kingdom forward, she made sure she got it. Women have been given a bad rap throughout history because of this one woman. We need to realize, however, that the spirit of Jezebel is part of the antichrist system that will try to arise in women to stop the move of God in the days ahead.

Women, you are about to come into conflict with a Jezebel spirit, and it is not in you; it's outside of you. You are going to have to stand and say: "Look at us, we will show you what God looks like." When we talk about the prophets of Baal being confronted, we had better get ready. We cannot fear the supernatural. We will be confronting a supernatural move of the devil through women in days ahead—women doing supernatural exploits that are not of God. Women of God will have to rise up into a greater anointing.

Jezebel represented a false apostolic movement. Therefore, what God is saying to the women is: "You must rise up now. If you will become devoted worshipers in this hour of the Church, I will change the course of this land." It is time for the accusation of Jezebel that has rested on women to leave. We must break that spirit and corresponding reproach so that the apostolic movement in women can move forward in days to come.

Snare #9: She allows circumstances to produce self-pity, causing her to miss her provision for the future.

In 1 Kings 17:9, God said to Elijah, "Arise, go to Zeraphath, which belongs to Sidon, and dwell there. See, I have commanded a widow there to provide for you." Just as God had said, a widow met Elijah at the city gates. Elijah said to her, "Please bring me a morsel of bread in your hand" (v. 11). So she said, "As the Lord your God lives, I do not have bread, only a handful of flour in a bin, and a little oil in a jar, and see, I am gathering a couple of sticks that I may go in and prepare it for myself and my son, that we may eat it, and die" (v. 12).

How's that for faith? She was so overwhelmed by her circumstances that she had no idea that provision was currently within her. God had already released the power of provision not only in her for her family, but for the prophet as well. However, the woman had not activated in her life what God had released from heaven. Women often do not see the level of provision that is already inside of them. They've been trained to depend upon others, so they do not creatively allow God to unlock His provision within them. There is a power of provision within women that needs to be tapped into like an oil well.

Right now we are about to see women move into a place of supernatural multiplication and provision like never before. Women are about to move out into the business centers of the earth and into government. In times of trial, women are going to have key wisdom over how to multiply. It is inside of you! Don't fall to the snare, "Oh woe is me! I'm going to die." Absolutely not. That is a snare from hell at this particular time in history. What God is saying to women is, "You have the creative ability within you to do exploits in days ahead." When the widow broke through the self-pity of her circumstances and gave the first fruit of her supply to the prophet, she had ample provision for her future.

Snare #10: She becomes distracted from the ultimate best that God has for her.

Finally, let's look at one incident in the New Testament. I believe it is something in which women are prone to be trapped.

In Luke 10, Jesus came to the house of Mary, Martha and Lazarus. During His visit, Mary sat and listened to Jesus and

gained the full benefit of His visit, while Martha was distracted with serving. Here is a major snare for women. Jesus
addressed Martha in this. He said to her, "Martha, Martha, *you
are troubled and worried about many things*" (Luke 10:41, emphasis
added).

Martha was distracted from what Jesus was doing in that
hour. I would say that the greatest snare I see for women is to
allow themselves to get distracted from what God is trying to
accomplish in their lives personally, as well as corporately and
territorially. Honestly, I want to say this to women: I don't
know how you do what you do. I travel 75 percent of the time.
When I go home and am there for two days, I marvel at all my
wife does. I don't know how she has any time to seek the Lord.
Every kid is pulling on her wanting something. She is trying to
keep the house straight, getting everyone and everything in
place, teaching, staying in touch with me, making sure I'm
taken care of (and I'm high maintenance) and she still does not
get distracted! This amazes me. Yet it is a snare for women to get
distracted.

This is not a time to get distracted, or you will miss the move
of God in the land. Dishes are necessary, chores are necessary,
the needs of your family are necessary; just don't allow them to
cause you to miss your visitation from the Lord.

JESUS CHANGES THE STATUS OF WOMEN

In the Old Testament under the Old Covenant, women were
essentially relegated to the status of keeping the home. But
because of God's sovereignty, He would raise up women leaders from time to time. When He did this, these women had an
incredible representation of the apostolic anointing. They
exercised great influence and, in some instances, ruled better

than the men of their time. God would break into a culture that subjugated women to men and raise women to positions of leadership.

In John 8, Jesus demonstrated what the Father in heaven was saying about women:

> Now early in the morning He came again into the temple, and all the people came to Him; and He sat down and taught them. Then the scribes and Pharisees brought to Him a woman caught in adultery. And when they had set her in the midst, they said to Him, "Teacher, this woman was caught in adultery, in the very act. Now Moses, in the law, commanded us that such should be stoned. But what do you say?" This they said, testing Him, that they might have something of which to accuse Him. But Jesus stooped down and wrote on the ground with His finger, as though He did not hear. So when they continued asking Him, He raised himself up and said to them, "He who is without sin among you, let him throw a stone at her first." And again He stooped down and wrote on the ground. Then those who heard it, being convicted by their conscience, went out one by one, beginning with the oldest even to the last. And Jesus was left alone, and the woman standing in the midst. When Jesus had raised himself up and saw no one but the woman, He said to her, "Woman, where are those accusers of yours?" (John 8:2-10).

People have been accusing the female ever since Eve ate the fruit. They have been finding every opportunity to accuse women. Now woman, look around. Where are your accusers? Jesus removed that mantle of accusation. It doesn't matter what you are prone to do, for Jesus has already addressed it on your behalf. Now He is saying, "Where is that accusation that says you can't control your desires; that you are the weaker sex who falls into deception; that your emotions are like a roller coaster? Where is that accusation that you are manipulative, controlling and have hidden agendas; that says you are a seductress? Where is that accusation that says you live under self-pity; are the weaker sex; and that you can't get focused, but rather get distracted? Woman, where are your accusers?"

God has brought us to this place because He is doing a new thing with women. Therefore, because He is doing a new thing, choose to have a clean slate. This is what He said to the woman in John 8. He said, "Has no one condemned you? . . . Neither do I condemn you; go and sin no more" (John 8:10-11). We are at such a historic juncture. God is saying, "I am putting my apostolic mantle on women." I don't know that He has ever fully said that since the Early Church. He is saying, "Let the condemnation of the past be removed from you. Let it go, so I can begin to use you in the way that I long to use you. This is a new day; I have a new way. I have chosen to move with women in a way that will change the course of the earth. You've made mistakes. Watch Me remove the power of the mistakes you have made in the past. You've fallen into all sorts of problems. Now watch Me begin to rip all of that off of you and clothe you with favor so that you can advance in a new way. It is a new day; it's a new way."

The first redemptive promise found in the Word of God is that although Satan would bruise woman's heel, she would crush his head. The enemy has so many women cowering down that they fear bruising their heel. Consequently, they lose sight of the fact that they are to crush the enemy's head. Women, now is the time to ask the Lord to make your heel strong. Shake off the bruising of your heel and confess that your heel is ready to crush the enemy's head!

WOMEN AWAKE!

This is a time of awakening. Deborah was a woman who woke up to God's purposes! As the *Dictionary of Biblical Imagery* puts it, "The general concept of 'awakening' captures the notion of either rousing oneself or being aroused in order to take action, as in the call of Deborah to 'wake up' in song (Judg. 5:12, *NIV*)."[5] Women, you are more important in God's future than you know.

In his book *Satan's Subtle Attack on Woman*, Dr. J. G. Morrison makes an appeal to liberated women to lead the way in devoted service and sacrifice for the One who has freed them from bondage:

> The advent of Jesus Christ saved womanhood . . . [Christian] women, do not forget your heritage. You are the spiritual descendants of the Sarahs, the Deborahs, and the Hannahs of the Old Covenant. Your line is renewed again in the New Testament in Mary who gave birth to Jesus Christ; Elizabeth who mothered His great forerunner; in Mary of Bethany, who anointed His precious head and feet; in Mary Magdalene, who was last at His cross and first at His empty tomb; in the host of women who in the early gospel days, gave their hearts, homes, and deepest toil to the cause of the Master. Your line is again renewed in church history, until for faithfulness, devotion, heroism, martyrdom and all else that pleases the heart of the great Christ, woman has along the way, borne the brunt, shared the vigils, preached with life and lip, and handed the cause on to the next age, with its banners proudly breasting every gale of opposition . . . Remember then, sisters, your marvelous heritage, and your amazing responsibility.[6]

We will not win the future war of the Church without women coming into their place. Now is the time, women of God, for you to understand your invaluable worth, come into the alignment God has for you and exercise the unique gifts and callings the Lord has for you at this strategic time in history. If you will do so, great victory lies ahead for the Church! Barbara Yoder is a perfect example of one who has responded to the call of God on her life. See how she stepped into her apostolic mandate, and how she is impacting the world around her.

CHAPTER 2

CAPTURED FOR DESTINY

Barbara J. Yoder

This book has not been written to defend a biblical position or a woman's right to do certain things. Many books have been written on those topics. This book is written with the conviction that the possibilities for women are limitless. The only thing that determines the boundaries of a woman's call is the Lord Himself and the personal mandate or mission He has given to her. This is a book that speaks to those "little girls" still hidden in time, space and culture, encouraging them to come out of their caves and attain all God intends for them. This is a book to call out women, young and old alike, to fully become the women God has ordained them to be, no longer dwarfed in spiritual fulfillment.

Women, dream on in God. Begin to translate your dreams into a mission. Begin to live out your mission in life with passion and confidence. God has made you to be co-equal participants in the apostolic mandate first set forth in Genesis and repeated by Jesus in His Great Commission. It was His final parting word to the 120, both men and women, in the book of Acts. This is a day to awake, arise, advance, penetrate and transform. This is a day to break through and break out of all that has restricted you![1]

HOW DID IT BEGIN?

How did it begin with me? I stood there alone—an innocent, naïve 11-year-old girl—after a church service next to the second row of gray folding chairs in that small, barren-looking building. Small for my age, I looked young and unimpressive. But there was very little that I did not observe. I watched intently as this gray-haired woman by the name of Roxie Kinnamon marched toward me. She was a woman on a mission; you could see it in her eyes. Though she was fixed on me and walked with determination, I was not frightened. Something inside me knew this woman, though I had not spent any time with her.

As I recall, she was older, but not elderly. I liked her and was drawn to her. She was close to God in a way most people were not, and I wanted that same thing for myself. When I got close to her, somehow I felt I got closer to God. I did not understand any of this at the time; after all, I was only 11. I remember that she stood in stark contrast to the church we attended. I did not like church—not this church anyway. I never wanted to go. Church made me sad, and I always struggled with feeling as if I were the worst sinner in the world. But I did want to be close to Roxie Kinnamon. There was something different about her.

And there she was, marching right towards me. On the way, she found my parents and brought them with her. When she got to me, she placed her hands gently on my shoulders and began to speak to my parents. She explained that a few days prior she had been praying and God spoke something to her that she needed to tell us. He told her, "This child is called to raise up a mighty work for God." What else she said that day, I don't remember. But those words replayed constantly in my head for years, and continued to speak to me, even when I thought I was an atheist.

What did those words mean? I could not get that woman or her words out of my head. Why? Because of the impact that encounter had on me. When Roxie Kinnamon put her hands on my shoulders, it was as if God Himself reached down and touched me. Years later, when I was so distant and removed from God, I could not get away from that touch or from what she had said. I constantly wondered about God and my future, even though I had not been around Roxie Kinnamon since I was 12. Little did I know that by her words, I had been captured for destiny.

CAPTURED BY GOD

In October of 1969, I was teaching at a university. My world was academics. Because of the intellectual atmosphere, as well as my search for answers, I was constantly studying the philosophers, both Christian and non-Christian. I thought I was searching for true reality; what I was actually searching for was God. So at night I would read, looking for something to fill the void. One night, I was alone in my bedroom sitting in the middle of my bed, reading Dietrich Bonhoeffer's book, *The Cost of Discipleship*.[2] I got to a chapter that spoke of the leap of faith. Something within me quickened and said, "Take the leap!"

I began to cry out, "God, if you exist, I have a few things to talk over with you." It was as if they were supernatural words. Something happened in my bedroom. Suddenly, Jesus walked into my room. When I saw Him, I became aware of His presence. I began sobbing uncontrollably as I looked at Him. I was overcome with absolute and unconditional love. It was as if a door within me that had been locked and sealed shut was suddenly opened and all the "stuff," the disappointments and disillusionments that had been stored up in my heart over the years, came tumbling out. That night I surrendered my life to God and became a Christian.

WHAT DID SHE MEAN?

I called my father the next night to tell him that I had become a Christian. He had been distraught by my alienation from God and the Church. I wanted him to know what had happened. After telling him the story, the first thing he said was, "Do you remember what Roxie Kinnamon told you?" I replied, "Dad, I have never been able to forget it." It was that night that I began a journey, not only in my personal relationship with God, but also in discovering the meaning of Mrs. Kinnamon's words.

Traditional, conservative, evangelical Christianity was my background. I had never found life in it, but it was the culture and belief system in which I had been raised. In fact, as a younger child, it was so void of life for me that I remember crying when I had to go to church and begging not to go. I hated it because I was drawn toward God, but I could never find Him. I felt like a spiritual failure and was sure I was predestined to hell.

My thinking and belief system were framed by the religious culture in which I was raised. All I could figure out from my background was that Roxie Kinnamon's words to me probably meant I would have to be a missionary. Women who answered "the call" became missionaries and disappeared in some country far away. When they came home, they would tell their story, ask us to help support them, and then they would go away again. That was what women did when they answered "the call." Is this what her words meant?

POSITIONED FOR PREPARATION

I ended up moving to Detroit and going to a church led by a woman. This woman had a mandate from God and had answered "the call." But, surprisingly, she had not disappeared into the hostile African jungle, which was my concept of missions at the time. She was a female pastor and preacher in a city in the United States of America. Not only that, she had raised up a church of 3,500 people! It was one of the five largest churches in America at the time. Though I had been a radical, hippie feminist, fighting for women's rights and positioning, I found I did not like her in the pulpit. What was a woman doing there? So for a whole year, I only went at night when her son spoke. Church tradition and culture had laid a foundation of belief within me that kept me from being able to fully perceive the plan of God.

Little did I know that God had led me there to begin to show me a picture of my future. But God first had to break through my mindset about women leading churches. This incredible leader, Myrtle D. Beall, and her daughter, Patricia Beall Gruits, became mentors to me, helping me to see there was more to answering "the call" than going to the African jungle. I have since been to Africa several times, and it is certainly not what I thought it would be. But at that time, I had a mindset framed by how I perceived the Church's teaching about women as well as missionaries' stories, pictures and artifacts. My beliefs and mindset were not framed by truth or by God and His Word.

DISCOVERING WHAT IT MEANT

It was there, at Bethesda Missionary Temple under the leadership of Myrtle D. Beall, that I began to connect with the call of God. I found out that to "raise up a mighty work for God" could mean many things. The church culture and tradition that had wrapped itself around me and kept me bound in a particular way of thinking began to be loosened off of me so that I could see the fullness of what that word might possibly mean. In time, I started to discover that for me, "the call" meant raising up a church that would not just be a local church, but would affect an entire region as well as the nations of the world.

Out of those simple and hidden beginnings, I began to discover a core vision, which then put mission into my life. That vision and mission began to shape my life and passion in a way that put definition to everything I did—even as concerned the people with whom I connected. God was in control. I began to uncover resources, people and relationships that caused the vision and mission that God had put within me to be loosed and propelled forward. Rivers of life from within were uncapped and passion began to light a fire that could not be put out. In fact, that fire burns even more brightly within me today.

I am a woman, culturally a white woman from a traditional conservative, evangelical background. But now I am also a prophet and apostle who now cannot sit down or shut up. For, like Jeremiah, something happened. A fire was loosed in my bones and I cannot shut up (see Jer. 20:9). The Word of God has lit a fire within me.

WHERE ARE THE APOSTOLIC WOMEN?

Where are the apostolic women whose fires have been lit by God, the movers and shakers? Awake and stand to your feet. This is a new day, and God is removing those things that have bound you and kept you encased in wrong mindsets and traditions. This is the day of the restoration of the Church of Acts, where women, along with men, will go forth to fulfill the call of God on their lives. Deborah, awake! Esther, take your place! Huldah, prophesy! Mary, conceive! This is a new day, one of empowerment and fulfillment.

The New Apostolic Reformation Church[3] has been birthed and is beginning to advance. Many are coming out of hidden places and going forth in the calling and anointing of God. This is a day when the calves are being let out of the stall, and they are going forth, leaping for joy because of the release (see Mal. 4:2). This is a day when those who have been the tail are coming out from behind and are taking their place side-by-side with those who have been in the front. This is the day of the Church—black and white, male and female, Jew and Gentile, slave and free, arising out of every tribe, tongue, people, nation and gender.

This is an awesome day—a day of freedom. Women, this is your day! In the next chapter we will begin to explore the apostolic mandate to which God is calling women in this hour.

CHAPTER THREE

SET FREE BY THE APOSTOLIC MANDATE

Barbara J. Yoder

Women were not created to just gather in some coffee house, department store, dining room or kitchen and come up with some activity to occupy their time. Women have been given their orders, commissioned and set free to accomplish their divinely-initiated destiny through the apostolic mandate. God spoke it in the beginning. He released an apostolic mandate to women, which defines the purpose of their existence and their destiny. They were not created to just hide behind a pile of dishes in a kitchen sink. Nor were they created to be lost in someone else's world. They were created to have significance and purpose, which is inherent in their destiny and in their apostolic mandate.

WHAT DOES APOSTLE AND APOSTOLIC MEAN?

What is the apostolic mandate? To understand, look first at the word "apostle." Strong's Dictionary defines the Greek word for apostle as a delegate, an ambassador of the gospel, or officially a commissioner of Christ with miraculous powers. In the King James Version of the Bible, it is also translated as a messenger or one who is sent.[1] So, an apostle is one who is sent and commissioned by God with miraculous power.

One may be a member of the Church but not necessarily an apostle. Because she is a member of the New Testament Church as set forth in Acts, she is therefore an "apostolic" believer. An apostolic believer is just as sent and equipped with miraculous power as an apostle. However, the authority to govern in and through the church (that is, the sphere and level of authority in which they operate) is different.[2] An apostle has the mantle to govern the church, whereas an apostolic believer is to govern her own life and that of her family (with her husband).

The Greek word for apostle is *apostello,* which means "set apart" and, by implication, to send out on a mission, literally or figuratively. It also is translated "to put in," "send" (away, forth, out) and "to set at liberty."[3] All believers are to be apostello—set apart and sent out by God to impart something to others and accomplish a mission within or outside of the church. They are also to be set at liberty and freed to go forth, as well as to liberate or free others. Part of the apostolic function is both to be set free and then to set others free. Women are to be set free within an apostolic structure and environment so that they can be sent forth with power and authority.

Mandates are acts or assignments entrusted to us by a higher authority. *Webster's Dictionary* says that a mandate is "an authoritative command, a formal order from a superior court or official to an inferior one, an authorization to act given to a representative, an order or a commission."[4] God gave to us a mandate that sets us apart from others and for which we are sent out to accomplish. We are to have an ambassadorial mandate to cause something to happen within the sphere of our assignment. An ambassador is a diplomatic agent of the highest rank who represents a government or sovereign that has sent and appointed such a one for a special assignment.[5] Therefore, an ambassador is an authorized representative or messenger.

In the book of Acts, a shift occurred. In chapter 2, the Church in Acts was birthed.[6] Women began to be actively recruited, included and empowered. The apostles not only addressed men but they also addressed women, which Luke referred to at times as both chief women and honorable women (see Acts 13:50; 17:4; 17:12). Furthermore, both men and women were bound, taken into custody and imprisoned for their faith, which means they were not sitting at home reading their Bible or watching television (see Acts

8:3; 9:2; 22:4). They were disturbing the peace of the religious structure that was in place. Women were included in prayer meetings (see Acts 1:14). Many women responded to the gospel and became believers (see Acts 5:14; 16:13; 8:12). And at least one woman was an apostle. Paul said in Romans 16:7, "Salute Andronicus and Junia, my kinsmen, and my fellow prisoners, who are of note among the apostles, who also were in Christ before me" (*KJV*). Junia was a woman.

In other words, both men and women were extraordinary. They were extraordinary because they were true believers who were radical about their faith. Once they were baptized in the Holy Spirit, a supernatural empowerment and boldness filled them. Women were apostolically empowered individuals who were called apart and sent out by God to accomplish a specific mission with miraculous powers; in other words, signs, wonders and miracles (the mighty deeds spoken of in 2 Corinthians 12:12). Not only were apostles called, sent out and empowered—the whole Church was as well. Jesus had said that when He was exalted to the right hand of the Father, His people would do greater works than He. He did not qualify His statement. "Most assuredly, I say to you, he who believes in Me, the works that I do he will do also; and greater works than these he will do, because I go to My Father" (John 14:12).

God gave a mandate to believers to go into the entire world and preach the gospel. Furthermore, He told them to make disciples, not of all people, but of all nations (see Matt. 28:12-19). Then in the beginning of Acts, God poured out His Holy Spirit (see Acts 1:8; 2), which caused people to be endued with such power that they were compelled to be witnesses as well as martyrs. They were witnesses in Jerusalem, then Judea, Samaria and the uttermost parts of the earth. There were no gender-qualifying statements. He was compelling *everyone* to go and to preach, teach, heal the sick, cast out demons and perform signs and wonders. He said believers would do these things in His name (see Mark 16:17-18). So, where did all of this begin?

MALE AND FEMALE CREATED EQUALS BY GOD IN THE GARDEN

The equality of men and women began in the Garden of Eden. God started it. There we find the original apostolic mandate. First, God created man. When He created man, He said "Let Us make man in Our image, according to Our likeness." (Gen. 1:26). Then He gave man (whom He referred to as "them") dominion over everything, including the earth. Scripture says He created them in His own image, which was both male and female (see Gen 1:26-27). Basically, this is what God said of Himself: "I am both male and female, man and woman, and I am making you like Me." After saying that, Genesis 1:28 states, "Then God blessed them, and God said to them, 'Be fruitful and multiply; fill the earth and subdue it; have dominion over the fish of the sea, over the birds of the air, and over every living thing that moves on the earth.'" This original mandate given to the human race was intended for both male and female, before there was such a thing as marriage and before they had a family.

FIRST APOSTOLIC MANDATE OUTLINED

Male and female were told to do five things in Genesis 1:28. God spoke to both of them simultaneously, giving them the same mandate. First, they were to be fruitful, which is to bear fruit, grow and increase. They were to reproduce not only themselves but everything they touched. Also, everything they put their hands to was to grow and increase. Second, God said they were to multiply or abound in everything. Third, they were to fill the earth, which means to furnish it; they were to make it look good, cause it to flourish and accomplish the purpose for which it was put in place.

Next He gave them two warring commandments—subdue and take dominion. God did not say, "male you do this and female you help him." They were both standing there when He spoke to *them*. So fourth, they were to subdue (tread down anything that arose against them or God), conquer it and bring under subjection that which was put under their care, which was everything. Finally, they were to rule the earth. God said they were to subjugate it, bring it under their control, reign and rule in and over it as well as prevail against anything that arose against them. They were God's delegated authority in the earth to run the earth for God.

To summarize, in the first chapter of Genesis both male and female were mutually given the responsibility for the earth and everything in it. It was only after and because of the Fall that God said to the woman that the man would rule over her (see Gen. 3:15-16). Woman now suffered from the curse; her desire shifted to her husband and the man was now to rule over her. However, as we saw in chapter 1, Jesus came to restore that which the first Adam gave over to Satan. Jesus became the second Adam to redeem us from the results (curse) of the first Adam's failure, the Fall, so that we could regain our pre-Fall authority and dominion (see 1 Cor. 15:43-50).

CALLED TO CO-LABOR WITH CHRIST

God is looking for a people who will become so redeemed that their spiritual perception will be restored and they will see as God sees. One word in the New Testament Greek for "hardness of heart" is translated as "to be destitute of spiritual perception."[7] In other words, we see with human eyes, naturally and not spiritually. God is longing for us to see as He sees. Paul said that the natural person does not receive the things of the Spirit (see 1 Cor. 2:14). God is looking for a people who will advance the kingdom of God in the earth, not just the Church. He is looking for women who will arise, go forth and take the dominion He gave to them in the beginning: to be co-laborers with Him and with men in redeeming and restoring humanity and the earth.[8] So within every woman is a call to labor with Christ in a specific area, increasing in and ruling over that which has been given to her. In Acts, women went everywhere preaching the kingdom of God.[9]

EMPOWERED BY THE HOLY SPIRIT TO INCREASE AND RULE

We see that God gave the original apostolic mandate in Genesis 1:28 to both male and female. He did not qualify it. So, Woman of God, arise and take your apostolic place in this hour. God not only called you to increase and take dominion, but He empowered you with the *dunamis* power. The word "dunamis" is a Greek word meaning force or miraculous power. It also means ability, abundance, might, power and strength.[10] This kind of strength refers to the power to withstand attack. You received the dunamis power of the Holy Spirit when you were baptized in His Spirit. Think of water baptism. One comes up fully covered, saturated and dripping with water. You, as God's woman, are fully immersed, saturated and dripping with the Holy Spirit's dunamis power. That dunamis power is the enabling power of God to do and become all that He has called you to. It is also the ability to demonstrate miraculous power—to perform miracles.

The word "dunamis" is inherent in Genesis 1:28 (and vice versa) because we are to increase, to abound and to take dominion. To take dominion is to rule where we are assigned. We are not to let the enemy rule us or our assigned territory, but we are to rule and release the kingdom of God where we are and wherever we go. Jesus said to us that the kingdom of God is within us (see Luke 17:21). That means it is here, right now, if we are in Christ and He is in us. Where the kingdom of God is, the rule of God is there also. For God is the king of the Kingdom. How do we rule and release His Kingdom? We do it by being saturated by the Holy Spirit.

We, as women, are to take our full apostolic authority in the place where we are assigned, simply because as believers we have been told to do so. All of us are assigned a certain sphere or boundary (see 2 Cor. 10:13-16) and are given authority over everything within the boundaries of our sphere. The psalmist said to us, "Rule in the midst of your enemies!" (Ps. 110:2). We have been empowered by the Holy Spirit to do just that.

ANOINTED WITH FRESH OIL

To be empowered is also to be anointed with fresh oil. David said in Psalm 92:10, "I have been anointed with fresh oil." *Barnes Notes* says this means oil that is pure and sweet, not old and rancid. As a result of being anointed, people would be made happy, cheerful, bright and prosperous. Anointing with oil in the East was the symbol of all this; it was equivalent to what we mean by putting on festive apparel—holiday apparel.[11] Like the oil, our experience with God is to be fresh, not an old experience.

Psalm 23:5 says, "You prepare a table before me in the presence of my enemies; You anoint my head with oil; my cup runs over." *Barnes Notes* says that in Hebrew, to anoint with oil is to make fat. That is, God pours oil on our heads so abundantly that it seems to be made fat with it. This expression in Hebrew indicates abundance. It is done on special occasions as an indication of prosperity and rejoicing and is indicative of divine favor, prosperity and joy.[12]

The word "anoint" means to smear with oil or grease. It causes us to shine. We shine with the glory of His presence resting upon us and within us. Anointing brings us into prosperity, favor with God and others, joy and abundance. In Isaiah 10:27, the prophet said that "It shall come to pass in that day that his burden will be taken away from your shoulder, and his yoke from your neck, and the yoke will be destroyed because of the anointing oil." In their commentary of the Old Testament, Keil and Delitzsch shed light on this by interpreting this passage to mean that the anointing causes fatness. [13] As the neck of the ox grows fat, the yoke is broken. Yokes represent restrictions. In every instance, anointing with oil represents being smeared or empowered with God's Spirit to abound, increase, prosper and release great joy. This breaks every narrow place or restriction that we face. Furthermore, we are able to slip through every narrow place and restriction because we have been smeared with oil. [14]

Women of God, we are anointed with fresh oil. Because of the fatness that the anointing has released, we are to prosper fully and go forth with joy to accomplish the apostolic mandate that is set forth before us. It is not a grievous mission, but one that will bring us into fulfillment with great joy, because we will go forth, smeared with fresh oil. We are greased so that every part functions smoothly, without friction or resistance. The Holy Spirit has been poured out upon us to empower us and grease us up to accomplish with great fulfillment that which is set before us. He anointed us with fresh oil so that we could accomplish the apostolic mandate with great joy.

APPREHENDED AND SENT OUT TO ACCOMPLISH A SPECIFIC PURPOSE

How each woman fulfills the mandate is specific to the vision given to her by God. We are sent out to accomplish something specific and we are furnished to do it. Vision comes out of times when God meets with us face to face to talk with us, inform us and show us what we are to do. Even when it comes out of a prophetic directive from another, there must be a time when that vision is transferred into our own heart through an encounter with God.

In Isaiah chapter 6, the prophet Isaiah had an overwhelming encounter with God. He was caught up into the presence of God and saw Him in all of His glory. He also saw the angels of God. In that encounter, Isaiah was awed by the glory of the presence of the Lord. He cried out that he was undone, a man of unclean lips, dwelling in the midst of a people of unclean lips (see v. 5). One of the seraphim came and cleansed his lips with a live coal, took away his iniquity and forgave Isaiah of his sin (see vv. 6-7). Following the cleansing, Isaiah then heard the Lord cry out, "Whom shall I send, and who will go for Us?" (v. 8).

In that encounter with God in all of His glory, an invitation was issued to Isaiah. God caused Isaiah to see into the very heart of heaven; to see Him, His majestic glorious domain and the angels ministering before the throne. It brought Isaiah to a place of brokenness where he became aware of his own depravity and inability to stand before God. That encounter also convinced Isaiah of his failure to qualify to do anything for God. When we see God as He is, we cannot but fall down before Him in humility and brokenness, feeling depraved and inadequate, realizing that we fall so short of His glory. Yet God in His mercy cleansed and forgave Isaiah. Then He called to Isaiah, "Whom shall I send, who will go for us?" God turned around and said, "Okay Isaiah, now I can challenge you with destiny in Me." This capturing of Isaiah into the glory of God was not just an experience to titillate him. It was a bringing of Isaiah into the presence of the Lord to prepare him and then impart a mandate to him.

God is looking for women who, through worship, will go up into heaven (see Rev. 4:1) and see God as He is. Seeing Him will break them to the core, showing them their own depravity and their inability to allow God to call them because of their depravity. Yet in that submission, God will come and transform both unqualified and disqualified women into women of destiny, called to arise and go forth with apostolic vision, fulfilling the apostolic mandate in Genesis 1:28. He took Ruth, a Gentile, and grafted her into the very lineage of Jesus. Jews were to have nothing to do with Gentiles. He took Rahab the harlot, who would be a modern day prostitute, and transformed and adopted her into His own people. Then He placed her in the lineage of Jesus, creating a way for those who do not in any way qualify except through the mercy of God and the shed blood of Jesus Christ.

We have no excuse. God leaves no woman out. He made a way for the least qualified and the most sinful. Ephesians 2:13 says, "But now in Christ Jesus you who once were far off have been brought near by the blood of Christ." Lift up your eyes and see God for who He is—a redeemer, restorer, an imparter of destiny and the One who has empowered you to fulfill the purposes of God, the apostolic mandate on women. Lift up your hands and worship the Lord, for He is merciful. Even when we have missed it, He restores our destiny. This is women's day. God is calling us out of every tribe, tongue, nation and people, and setting us on our feet as never before to go forth. He is sending us forth to change the world. We are set free and commissioned by the apostolic mandate!

CHAPTER 4

APOSTOLIC PIONEERING

Wanda Studdard

I am a woman, I am an apostle. I am an African American. And, I am a pioneer with my husband, Apostle G. E. Studdard. We are planting and establishing new ministries that are impacting individuals, neighborhoods and cities. And God, through us, is going beyond race and gender to do it!

WHAT? A FEMALE APOSTLE?

For me, it started on February 3, 1987, around 9:00 P.M. I was in the home of Jim and Bonnie Kahn, in my hometown of Memphis. I had just finished teaching a Bible study class in their home when Jim began to prophesy and lay hands on me. He was sending me off from Memphis to Indianapolis to obey the call of God on my life. As I rejoiced over the word of the Lord to me, Bonnie walked up to me and said something I will never forget: "Wanda, the Holy Spirit said you are going to Indianapolis as an apostle of God, and when you return from Indianapolis, there will be a man with you who will love you greatly." It was easy for me to believe the part about a man, but I was hesitant to believe the part about being an apostle because I wasn't sure I believed women could be apostles. I told this to Bonnie, and she laughed and said, "Well you are one, a female apostle." From that point forward, Bonnie's words, "You're going to Indianapolis as an apostle of God," stayed with me.

I didn't realize at that time that I was not only going to Indianapolis to begin a new ministry, but I was being "sent" by God as an apostle. I was to be a delegate ambassador of the gospel to deliver a specific message to a specific people in a specific city. The journey had just begun.

JUNIA, A WOMAN APOSTLE

The question I had to answer was, "Does God call women to be apostles?" My answer was initially found in Romans 16:7. It says, "Salute Andronicus and Junia, my kinsmen, and my fellow prisoners, who are outstanding among the apostles, who also were in Christ before me" (*KJV*). I found that in the Greek language, "Junia" is a feminine word suggesting that she was a woman.[1] It also states she was an apostle in Rome. Josephus, a noted first-century historian, taught that Junia was the wife of Andronicus and that they went forth as apostles doing the works of God.[2] Romans 16:7 also indicates that Junia was not only a woman, but that she was outstanding among the apostles. Furthermore, in Genesis 1:28, God Almighty, the Creator of heaven and earth, gave both men and women the command to take dominion over the earth and the task of subduing it. Understanding this, I knew the same was true for me.

MY UNIQUE ROLE AS AN APOSTLE

As an apostle, I realize I play a unique role in establishing the Church. The Spirit of God gives me strategic battle plans through prayer to conquer or subdue the spirits that are assigned to a particular region. As a result, I am able to accomplish things in the realm of the spirit, much like Paul when he went into Ephesus in Acts 19.

While in Indianapolis, my presence as an apostle in the church brought strength to that work. God used me to deliver His Word to build up a firm foundation of instructional training that helped mature the saints to become more productive citizens in the Kingdom work in that city. He also used me to help the church come to a place in praise and worship that brought the people into contact with the glory of God. I have found that churches that have tapped into an apostolic anointing can release the power and presence of the Holy Spirit in their worship. It changes the spiritual atmosphere, releases a prophetic presence and opens people up to the Word of God.

FACILITATING CHANGE

My husband often refers to me as a troubleshooter. Between 1987 and 1989, the Holy Spirit sent me into five local churches to work with the pastors to bring change. Numerical, financial and spiritual growth occurred in all of them. During this time, I began to understand that the ability to discern and facilitate change is a part of my apostolic anointing. I locate hindrances in a church and provide the people with solutions that cause them to move into spiritual maturity and numerical growth.

In 1988, the Holy Spirit began to speak to me about Jeremiah 1:10: "See, I have this day set you over the nations and over the kingdoms, to root out and to pull down, to destroy and to throw down, to build and to plant." Watching how He worked through me, I knew it was another aspect of my apostolic anointing. In the churches where I was sent, the apostolic anointing worked to root out, pull down, destroy and throw down the works of darkness in the lives and mindsets of people, and then to build their lives by planting the Word of God in them. However, like the apostle Paul, I too have had to labor in prayer so that the saints I work with will be matured and complete in the will of God (see Gal. 4:19). I enforce living a holy life and walking in righteousness. I bring light to those in darkness through my teaching ministry.

TRAILBLAZERS AND PATHFINDERS

According to *Webster's Dictionary*, to pioneer means to progress or to gain ground.[3] Apostles are pioneers. My husband and I are trailblazers and pathfinders. We are taking the lead by initiating reformative action in the lives of people and in the atmosphere of a region. We break through ignorance, fear and other obstacles that keep the Church from advancing. When sent to a church, we equip them to become effective in releasing the kingdom of God through evangelism, teaching and anointed praise and worship.

The book of Joshua demonstrates our type of apostolic leadership. Joshua stood in the face of opposition and influenced his domain. He was able to motivate the people to possess the inheritance given to them by God (see Josh. 3—6). He was not passive. He broke through. Similarly, God has called our ministry to take command, clothed in His armor, redeeming people for His glory, and possessing the land He has given us. And we are doing it. We are a type of the Joshua generation.

WALKING IN APOSTOLIC AUTHORITY

In order for the Body of Christ to function in the dominion and authority it has been given, I believe we must all walk in our God-given, apostolic anointing. Jesus had a mandate to fulfill and He fulfilled it. He took dominion over the weather and brought it under control, He subdued and conquered sickness and disease, and He raised the dead.[4] Like Jesus, my husband and I have had to break through cultural, racial and natural barriers to function in our apostolic calling. We are bringing the presence of God wherever God sends us!

Any Christian, male or female, can operate in this same type of authority. However, we must receive instruction from the Father the same way Jesus did. I have learned that operating in this type of authority comes when we hear and obey His voice. Creative miracles and raising the dead come *only* when we exercise authority and dominion over the things in which the Spirit of God instructs us. I have had to learn the importance of being directed by the Holy Spirit in order to walk in the fullness of my calling. As a five-fold minister, I believe I have even more responsibility to tap into His leading because of the unique role I play in helping establish the Church.

What I realized early on was that the real us is spirit. Our "earth suit," or body, should not determine what we can or cannot accomplish for our Lord, Jesus of Nazareth. Any born-again Christian who knows and believes the Word of God pertaining to dominion and authority will not sit around and let the enemy raise havoc in any area of his or her life. When our spirit is born-again, it takes on the nature of our Heavenly Father, which is the life of God (see John 3:5-6). The real us is spirit!

UNFOLDING THE APOSTOLIC CALL

During our time in Baton Rouge, when God was unfolding the apostolic call on my husband and me, we began to be sought out by others to provide apostolic leadership, counsel and spiritual covering. One time, after being approached by a certain couple, G. E. and I just looked at each other and shrugged our shoulders. We didn't know what to do with them, but thought, "Okay, Lord, if this is what you want, we will be apostles over them."

Today, regardless of where the Lord sends us or what the assignment is, supernatural manifestations of God are released. Churches are changed. People are added to the Church, finances begin to flow in abundance, and the saints are strengthened and encouraged.

Even Harvest Prayer Center in Baton Rouge, a sister work to our church in Indianapolis, is an apostolic work that we pioneered in 1996. It is not large numerically, but it has given us an avenue to make progress in the spirit realm of the city. It took me a while to realize that our results had a great deal to do with the apostolic anointing and mandate that was on our lives.

NEW UNDERSTANDING

Hosea 4:6 says, "My people are destroyed for lack of knowledge." Praise God that my thinking changed because of the knowledge I received about the apostolic calling! With the understanding of the authority I walk in now, even demons recognize my calling! As a woman, it is an honor to be called of God to stand in the office of an apostle. May every tribe and tongue be represented before His throne as a result of what He is doing through men *and* women today!

CHAPTER 5

THE POWER OF
THE SEED

Barbara J. Yoder

Women are full of seeds—powerful seeds that have the capability of changing the earth in which they live. A seed is one of the most important and powerful substances on Earth. It has the power to reproduce itself and overtake the place where it is planted. Furthermore, once it germinates and reproduces itself in one place, it can spread to other places. Ultimately, it has the potential to fill the entire Earth with its substance. Within women are seeds that contain the spiritual DNA essential to accomplish the apostolic mandate.

Every person, regardless of gender, contains seeds. A seed is the matter essential to begin something. Without seeds life cannot begin, be it human, ideological or botanical. There is seed that produces natural offspring; children who have within them a mandate from God. A seed may also produce ideas, vision, assignments and connections, which have the power to change whatever that seed begins to penetrate. Scripture calls the Word of God seed that, when planted, has the power to produce what the Word declares (see Isa. 55:10-11; Mark 4:3-20).

DESTINED TO CRUSH SATAN'S HEAD AND POSSESS GATES

In Genesis 3, God cursed Satan in the Garden and declared something powerful to the woman. He said in Genesis 3:15, "I will put enmity between you and the woman, and between your seed and her Seed; He shall bruise your head, and you shall bruise His heel." Within woman and her seed is the power to crush the head of Satan, the controlling structure that brings individuals, societies and cities into devastation and captivity (see Isa. 14:12-17).

In Genesis 24, Rebekah's family blessed her when she was getting ready to leave to marry Isaac. They said something very important to her in that blessing. They said that her *seed* would possess the gates of those who hate her (see Gen. 24:60, *KJV*). What an extraordinary thing to say! In other words, there was something powerful about women's seed, or at least about Rebekah and her seed. But stop right here! Remember that this statement had already been made to Abraham in Genesis 22:17. So this blessing extends back in time, before Rebekah. Yet it starts with her as the one who gave birth to the next generation that was called to inherit the blessings of Abraham. It was not just her seed, but it belonged to Isaac as well, and it affected grandchildren and great-grandchildren along with thousands of descendants.

Now move forward in history. Let's look at what Paul said in Galatians 3: "That the blessing of Abraham might come upon the Gentiles in Christ Jesus, that we might receive the promise of the Spirit through faith. Brethren, I speak in the manner of men: Though it is only a man's covenant, yet if it is confirmed, no one annuls or adds to it. Now to Abraham and his Seed were the promises made. He does not say, 'And to seeds,' as of many, but as of one, 'And to your Seed,' who is Christ" (vv. 14-16).

This passage extends what is said in Genesis to Abraham all the way to the Gentiles in the New Testament, who were grafted into the vine through Christ Jesus. If that isn't clear, then Paul adds verse 29, which says, "And if you are Christ's, then you are Abraham's seed, and heirs according to the promise." That being the case, we are Abraham's seed and, therefore, are full of seed, both male and female. That seed is intended to possess the gates of the enemy, to overcome, overtake and multiply until it fills the earth. It is the very glory of God manifested through His people and filling the earth (see Hab. 2:14).

WHAT IS SEED?

What is seed? Why is it so powerful? How is it powerful? If we understand what seed is, then we will understand the fullness of the potential in one seed. Furthermore, we will understand why seed is so threatening to the enemy and how powerful it is in the hands of God.

First of all, a seed is just a small kernel, a germ. But living within it is the power of reproduction. If the seed is fertilized and then planted, it will reproduce that which it came from. Furthermore, in the plant that results, the original seed exponentially reproduces multiplied seeds. Jesus used the seed as an example of multiplication when He said, "Unless a grain of wheat falls into the ground and dies, it remains alone; but if it dies, it produces much grain" (John 12:24). In other words, if it is planted in the ground, it will reproduce.

A seed is the beginning or starting point. Every human being is the result of a seed from both parents. Every ministry, project, program or initiative begins with a seed. Seeds are powerful because they start something. Men and women are filled with seeds. The Word or purpose of God is planted in us at creation. Seeds are propagating structures.

To propagate is to cause something to be proliferated, spread out or disseminated. That is very similar to the verb for seeding, which means to cover or permeate by scattering something. It means to bear fruit, multiply and fill the earth. Furthermore, it goes beyond the natural realm to the spiritual realm. Women have seeds in them which, when germinated, create and multiply offspring. They have the power to overcome whatever would get in their way or try to obstruct their growth.

Tonya Roberson, a leader in our church who is called to be an apostle, had a *seed*—a vision to see men in prison redeemed and transformed. She formulated, developed and launched that ministry. Now, she is reproducing herself and multiplying this effort by developing others to reach men for Christ in a federal prison. As a result, prisoners are coming to Christ. They are being transformed. A woman was given a seed that is now overcoming the gates of the enemy in federal prison.

Janice Patrick, another ordinary woman in our church, worked with mentally challenged individuals. She had a heart for these people and saw an opportunity to buy a halfway house. There was a seed of ministry inside of her. She bought the house and is now ministering to a select group of people, seeing miracles of breakthrough in their lives. Now she is expanding to a second house. Already she has another seed within her that has started to sprout. When listening to a report about men in prison, she decided that she was going to plan to develop a safe place of transition for men coming out of prison. Although this house is not in operation yet, the seed has sprouted and is beginning to grow. It is in the developmental process and will be transplanted from a seedling to a full-fledged ministry in three years.

These are ordinary women with seeds that cause them to see what others cannot see. Because they took a risk and sowed their seeds, not only have their ministries changed the quality of individuals' lives, but also the people themselves have been changed.

WHAT DO SEEDS DO?

Seeds release and stimulate growth and development. That means there is power within them that causes them to break into something new. True seeds from God don't just germinate and remain seedlings—they grow and develop. One seed from God starts as something very tiny—even invisible—but it has the potential to grow and develop to such an extent that it overcomes whatever is in its way. It will grow in the stature of Christ. It will grow in spiritual revelation, insight, understanding, wisdom and knowledge. It will grow in character and begin to look like Jesus. Part of the apostolic office (which is a type of seed) is to grow people into all things in Christ, who is the head of all (see Eph. 4:11-15).

Seeds are filled with life. They possess the very nature of Christ Himself. Christ is the seed or descendant of God. He is the Son of God. In Him is life, and that life is the light of all people (see John 1:4). Where seeds of God are released and begin to grow, life invades death and light overtakes darkness. Resurrection and revelation break out.

Seeds produce descendants. They produce children, grandchildren, great grandchildren and so forth. Part of the strategy some religions implement to gain adherents to their faith is through human reproduction. God promised Joshua that in each place his foot tread upon, He would give that land to Joshua. Islamic people believe this also, which is one of the reasons they are advancing as a world religion. We, as apostolic women, have the potential to birth children who will change the world. Our children are to go into all the world, touch their feet on the ground of nations, and believe God to give them nations.

OUR RESPONSE

We, as women, need to believe this. We need to begin to birth children with our husbands, proliferate ministries and create and grow new programs. We need to develop strategies that will grow people for the purposes of God. Seeds develop and grow into people and things. They produce outcomes and products. As a result of the seeds being released, germinated and developed, there are followers, disciples and successors.

Women around the world, in all sects of life, are arising and taking their place. From the homemaker to the CEO, from the Sunday School teacher to the pastor preaching in the pulpit every Sunday, women are arising and changing the world. They have followers who are true disciples, and they are mentoring successors.

Dr. Naomi Dowdy is a woman apostle who leads a great church in Singapore called Trinity Christian Center. Before going to Singapore to serve as the senior pastor, Dr. Dowdy served as an Assemblies of God missionary in the Marshall Islands. Now she leads one of the most significant churches in Singapore, consisting of 4,500 members. She is not ordinary. She is a very extraordinary woman, discipling leaders all over the world so that they can propagate the Church through the cell church concept. Dr. Dowdy is more than a local pastor; she is an international apostle leading other apostles. She works with Dr. C. Peter Wagner to help move the apostolic church forward. She gathers apostles from all over Southeast Asia to break through and further the growth of the church in that region of the world. Furthermore, she mentors those who can duplicate what she is doing, so that they can succeed her in time.

This extraordinary woman also is the founder and president of Global Leadership Network. Through this network, she comes alongside of churches and ministries to help them transform the harvest field into what she refers to as the "harvest force." Dr. Dowdy is recognized as one of Singapore's most sought after speakers. She is a dynamic leader whom God has graced with strong motivational skills. She conducts leadership training and church leaders around the world call upon her for advice. She empowers leaders across all five continents. She is a woman full of apostolic vision. She is a woman apostle, a great woman in (and of) God. Years ago, there was a seed within her.

She found it, nurtured and multiplied it, and now it is filling the earth.

MIRACULOUS MULTIPLICATION

The seeds in one apple can be counted. They can be cut out of the apple, laid on a piece of paper and numbered. However, there are so few seeds in one apple that most people never give them any thought, other than to remove them before eating the apple. But think about it—in one apple there are an exponentially multiplied number of apples that are produced from just a few seeds. One seed is jam packed with incalculable apples. Yet what we see is seemingly insignificant—a single seed. What would happen if we begin to tap into just a few of the seeds that are within us—or even just one seed? *How powerful it would be!*

The seed of a woman is meant to possess the gates of the enemy. It is to be released in the home, marketplace, government, judicial systems, schools, businesses and so forth. I recently read an article in *Fortune Magazine* about women and their husbands.[1] Women are going to work and impacting the world in very significant places. No longer is a woman's only option to stay at home. She can be whatever her drive, education, ability and talent enable her to be as never before.[2] Women, whether believers or not, are now going into all sectors of society of the world. Can you imagine the impact this would have on the world if this new company of women were Christians with an apostolic mind-set? I heard Dr. C. Peter Wagner talk about Linda Rios Brook. She is a Christian entrepreneur and apostolic pioneer in the marketplace who bought a defunct television station for around 3 million dollars and later sold it for 56 million dollars. She is currently spearheading the marketplace ministry branch, called LifeWorks, for Dr. C. Peter Wagner and Wagner Leadership Institute.

Another article in this same edition of *Fortune Magazine* was titled "True Grit." It captured the heart of God for Christian business leaders. The article started out by saying, "For the most powerful women in business, character matters now more than ever."[3] Sally Krawcheck headed a research department and business that faced off with Wall Street. She refused to go into investment banking or exotic trading. Her reason was because she wanted to give upright and conflict-free investment advice to people. For some time it looked like she would lose business and fail. Yet today, this woman is on *Fortune Magazine*'s list of the 50 Most Powerful Women in Business in America.[4] Whether Ms. Krawcheck is a believer or not, the article exemplifies how apostolic leadership will institute the standards of character for leaders in business and hold them to those standards. That leadership will in time bear great results, because people can trust it. Women leaders with great seeds are arising and propagating great products and outcomes.

I remember driving a car with a starter button as a kid. Press that button and the motor would start, causing the car to begin to operate and move forward. Seeds are like starter buttons in those old cars. Seeds start something. They cause something or someone to come into being. They activate something and it begins to operate and function. Seeds break something nonexistent into existence. They start a new course or begin a new journey. They initiate new activities and undertakings. As a result, that which has been hidden comes out of a place of concealment and develops form, shape and identity. Something begins to move, act or operate because a seed starts something.

WOMEN'S SEED MAKES A DIFFERENCE

Women are ordained by God to make a difference. Their function is unique. They take seed; and when that seed is fertilized, nurture it to birth in a protected or hidden place. Women take groceries and produce a meal. Women take household decorative items and furniture and produce a home. Women take ideas and develop programs that cause troubled children to come into significance and destiny. Women are arising who will catch vision and build businesses that change society. Women have a seed of intelligence and talent. They can go to college and gain knowledge and expertise, incubating what is within them. They can become doctors, lawyers, leaders of churches or even start new movements for God that will become new denominations. Women can become powerful and filled with destiny if they will do something with the seed of potential that is within them.

What if a woman never fully realizes what God has placed within her? She goes merrily on her way not even realizing the fullness of God within her. She has no idea of the mark of destiny within her seed. The seeds within her are hidden and concealed. Women have apostolic destinies and missions, but they remain covered, undiscovered and without identity. I believe this is part of Satan's strategy to keep women veiled, hidden and lacking connections that will cause them to start something. It is a planned deception to keep them from knowing who they are. As a result, they have no idea that God has commissioned them to go into all of the world and preach the gospel, making disciples of all nations. They are left with questions such as: What is my world? Where am I assigned? What am I to preach? What is my gospel? What is my mission? The answers often remain in seed form, hidden in a packet, waiting for spring to arrive. Who will open the packet and start planting the seeds?

WHAT ARE WOMEN?

Women are birthers. Part of their apostolic destiny is to see their seed through to full birth. Without women, there will never be a harvest. They must come alongside men and begin to labor with them so that the fullness of the harvest can come. Until women get in their place, the harvest will be withheld. Children do not come out of fathers; they come out of fathers and mothers. Mothers incubate and birth the seed into infancy. Then together, the father and mother raise the infant to full stature. What would happen in the church if women got into place? Could it be that then the harvest will break forth?

Women are travailers. In other words, when they see that it is time for something to spring into life, they labor over delivering the seed into life outside of the womb. They are made this way. Their body reacts physically at the time of birthing. Powerful chemicals are released to induce birth. There is an agony in women until the birth occurs. Women travail not only naturally, but spiritually, to see the seeds of God come forth into being.

Women are mothers. Their hearts are broken when there is no child. Proverbs 30:15-16 says that a barren womb is never fully satisfied. Barrenness never lets go of the heart of a woman. Hannah cried out to Eli because she was barren. Then Samuel was born (see 1 Sam. 1). Samuel was a firstborn child, holy to the Lord. He broke through his mother's womb, and with that breakthrough came seven more children. She was in a war over her seed. Until she broke through, destiny was thwarted. It created agony, and so she cried out in travail over her childlessness.

There is always war over the first child because once the womb is opened, more seed can be received and released. The firstborn child is so significant to God that He speaks about it in Exodus 34:19: "All that open the womb ["matrix" in the *King James Version*] are Mine, and every male firstborn among your livestock, whether ox or sheep." The firstborn child in the Old Testament received a double portion of his father's inheritance.

And he opened the womb; he started the germinating process and caused his mother to break through barrenness. There is a war over the first of anything.

BATTLE TO BREAK THROUGH

There is a battle over the seed to keep it from ever coming into its destiny. The enemy wants to keep women veiled, ignorant, deceived and hopeless. He wants them hidden, without a future and a hope. For when women break through, great things come into existence. They are called to do great exploits; they are apostolic.

Barbara Wentroble, a cutting-edge, breakthrough woman with a powerful apostolic call and anointing, went with a group of women to Afghanistan as a health consultant while United States troops were still there and bullets were riveting through the streets. She arrived in Kabul with her team just after the nation had been freed from the Taliban. Read this testimony that she wrote for me regarding a spiritual breakthrough that occurred while they were there.

Our team of five women arrived in Kabul, Afghanistan, May 20, 2002. The women in the city either had their heads covered with scarves or with burkas. Most covered their heads with the blue burkas.

Several days later, our team decided to sing a song and dance as a prophetic act of removing the burkas and bondages from the women of Afghanistan. "We're having a party," we sang. "Dancing with the Father, casting out demons, everywhere we go." As we sang, we threw the scarves from our heads to the floor. We danced on them as we sang. It seemed like a silly song and dance to those who did not understand the power of prophetic acts. To us, it seemed like the most powerful thing we could do!

Almost three weeks later, we left Afghanistan. At that time we noticed about 10 percent of the women on the Kabul University campus had removed their burkas. Six months later, other teams observed that about 90 percent of the women on the campus had removed their burkas. Some may think it was a coincidence. However, for those who released the prayer of faith with the prophetic acts of song and dance, it was the outward manifestation of God's liberating power for the women of that nation.

God is taking off the veils that have hidden women's true calling and destiny. This story is not only prophetic of what God was and is doing in Afghanistan, but also of what He is doing throughout the world and within the Church. This is a day of unveiling and releasing. God is uncovering and releasing the seed of destiny within every woman. As a result, women will come forth in increasing measure in the homes, marketplaces, government, schools, churches and businesses where God has assigned them. May that birthing, breakthrough anointing be released within them to break the strategies of the enemy to thwart the Church and its destiny from coming into fulfillment. This is the day for them to stand in their full apostolic authority and rule.

EVERY WOMAN IS A MOTHER

Perhaps the most influential and often overlooked aspect of a woman is the mothering nature within her. It is one of the keys to her apostolic positioning. It is part of her seed of destiny and is the unique apostolic character given to her. Men are fathers; women are mothers. I remember how powerful my mother was in my own life. Mothers are protectors, comforters, encouragers and exhorters; visionaries who take seed in partnership with their husbands, birth it and raise that child into an adult who will change their part of the world. Women don't have to be married or have babies to be mothers. Henrietta Mears was never married, yet she was a powerful woman who seeded destiny through her teaching and encouragement into such people like Bill Bright. Bill Bright birthed and developed Campus Crusade for Christ into one of the most influential and successful campus ministries in the world. Mears herself birthed Gospel Light, an evangelical publisher of which Regal Books is a ministry. The seed that was in her has now, even after her death, gone on to produce much fruit. She was a mother.

SEED OF DISCERNMENT

Another seed in women is their ability to discern. They have keen spiritual perception and discernment. However, since the enemy hates discernment because it uncovers his traps, snares and hidden strategies, he will use deception to cloud their ability to discern. Eve, the first woman, was deceived and entered into sin. The enemy targeted the gift within her. He directly attacked her redemptive identity as a discerner by tricking her. When women come alongside men and release their gift to discern, the two become much stronger and more effective than either one alone. Men need women and women need men. Their partnership will bring the Church into the fullness of its destiny. Seed cannot come into being without both a father and a mother. We need each other.

Revelation 12 gives us a picture of how much the enemy hates the woman's seed. The picture in Revelation directly relates to the Church. However, it also demonstrates the significance of a woman's seed to Satan. He is after her seed. Within her seed is the very presence of the person of Christ, who has already overcome every enemy. When a woman brings seed to birth that is out of the heart and call of God, it has the very nature of Christ within it. Satan hates that. Why? Because that seed has the power to overcome everything in its path. It is ultimately destined to succeed, because it is born of God in spite of all opposition against it (see 1 John 5:4).

POWER TO POSSESS

Women are seed bearers, destined to possess the gates of the enemy. Their seed has the power to dethrone. In days ahead, we are going to see this half of God's army arise in an unprecedented manner as we get closer to the end of the age. This is a new day. With this arising, understand that new opposition will also break out. Women must therefore have an apostolic identity and live according to that identity. For the very nature of the apostolic church in the book of Acts was that no matter who or what broke out against it, it did not pull back, quit, sit down or shut up. Within its DNA was God the Breaker (see Mic. 2:13), who overcomes every obstacle and hindrance. Apostolic seeds of destiny, not only in men but also in women, are being released to dethrone all that has raised itself up against the rule and reign of our Lord and Savior, Jesus Christ. What a day we live in!

Seeds demand a response. In the next chapter you will read how the *seed* put pressure on one woman, Jean Hodges, until she responded to the call of God. It's never too late to germinate the seed!

CHAPTER 6

IT'S NEVER TOO LATE TO ANSWER GOD'S CALL

Jean Hodges

Recently I visited a butterfly farm and was amazed as I watched thousands of beautiful lacy-winged, brilliantly colored insects flutter from flower to flower. We were told how they go through stages of change, first as caterpillars, who eat with voracious appetites then cocoon themselves away, and are in time transformed into the lovely creatures that emerge to fly thousands of miles, cross-pollinate plants and fulfill their destinies.

For many seasons women have been relegated to the worm stage and have been oppressed and suppressed by cultures, wrong attitudes, mores and religious systems. In this new season, the Lord is feeding His handmaidens with the truth of the Word of God. He is cocooning them in His love and beginning to transform them, to heal them of old wounds and to redeem them to the full purpose for which He designed them. Butterflies look very fragile, yet they are extremely strong, able to traverse continents and overcome many obstacles. In this new season, the Lord is bringing forth women of all colors and nationalities, infused with His Spirit, who are called to reflect His beauty, to demonstrate His love, to proclaim His message and to release His power in all the nations of the world.

LIBERATED FROM OPPRESSION

Last year, a documentary produced by a young English woman was aired on CNN. Her father was an Afghan who told her of the beauty of Afghanistan as he remembered it from his youth. He described the devastation of years of war and the extreme oppression of the Taliban. Desiring to expose the situation, she donned a burka and went into Afghanistan with a camera hidden under her clothing. She videotaped women imprisoned in the burka peering out through the tiny mesh opening over their eyes. Women spoke of being stripped of their identity, voice and usefulness in society. She interviewed professional women, doctors, lawyers and teachers who were forbidden to hold jobs. No woman was allowed to leave her home or go outside without male accompaniment. Many were widows because of the war, and many were mothers who in desperation to feed their children would sneak out under the cover of night to gather bread from the garbage dumps. She actually videotaped a woman being led into a soccer stadium, forced to kneel, and shot for some infraction of Taliban law while the male crowd stood cheering.[1]

As I watched in horror with tears in my eyes, I began to get a revelation of how much Satan hates women. I sat stunned at the full impact. Only a demonic force could perpetrate that kind of evil. Recently I heard Chuck Pierce say, "Look for the antichrist spirit where you see anti-Semitism and anti-women movements." That night the program, through her lens, brought the enmity between the Serpent and the woman into clear focus. God Himself prophesied this hatred in Genesis 3:15 when He said to the Serpent, "I will put enmity between you and the woman."

LIBERATED BY HOLY SPIRIT BAPTISM

As I contemplated the depth of that hatred, I was reminded of an experience I had many years earlier. My husband, Jim, was pastoring a denominational church whose previous pastor had to resign because he had received the baptism in the Holy Spirit. In order to protect our church, Jim began to study all he could on that topic and started attending Full Gospel Business Men's meetings. Having been taught that Spirit baptism was a dangerous doctrine, possibly opening a person up to the devil's deception, I was alarmed. It became my "mission" to protect him from this "heresy." I argued and criticized him relentlessly. One night I said to him, "speaking in tongues is the work of the devil." He had always been kind, never arguing back, but that time he looked at me with tears in his eyes and said: "Jean, be careful that you do not blaspheme the Holy Spirit." If he had thrown a literal sword, it could not have pierced me any deeper than his words did! My breath was taken away as this powerful word of God penetrated my heart and mind. I was stopped in my tracks and began to consider that quite possibly I might be wrong. I did not want to be guilty of the sin of blasphemy, and I surely did not want to miss God's truth. I asked the Lord to forgive me and teach me about the working of His Holy Spirit.

Over the next few months I began to see the truth of God's Word and became hungry to receive the Holy Spirit baptism. One day, Jim and I attended a Full Gospel Business Men's meeting where Kenneth Hagin was speaking. He taught on receiving the Holy Spirit, and I was one of the first to go forward. I was very expectant that this would be "my day" to receive the gift of tongues. He laid hands on me and prayed, but nothing happened. I did not begin to speak in tongues as I was sure I would. Kenneth Hagin was well known as a man of faith. I was convinced that if he laid hands on me and nothing happened, I must be a hopeless case! Remembering all the months of antagonizing my husband, I was afraid God was withholding that blessing from me.

Finally, at Jim's urging, we left the auditorium. When we stepped into the foyer, we saw David DuPlessis, a wonderful, elderly minister. Jim made the introduction and began to tell him how disappointed I was that I had not received the baptism that morning. I was rather chagrined that Jim was giving him that information, but soon I was overjoyed at what the Lord did.

David DuPlessis turned to me, took my hands and looked into my eyes. He began to instruct and encourage me in the Lord. As I looked into his eyes they suddenly changed. They seemed to become three dimensional and darker with a purplish color surrounding them. It was as if powerful waves of liquid, awesome, mighty love flowed from them into my soul and spirit. I began to cry as I was touched and ministered by the Holy Spirit. There was no condemnation, only overpowering life-giving love! What an experience! It forever changed me and I felt that Jesus Himself had been with me that day. How He must long for all women to know the magnitude and power of His love for them!

LIBERATED FROM PAST ENTRAPMENTS

Satan's desire is to keep women bound in a cocoon of intimidation, trapped in a burka of oppression, hiding under the bruises of abuse, shrouded in apathy and misunderstanding, unaware of God's call upon them. In this new season of restoration, the Lord has begun to strip away the demonic cocoon and is bringing liberation! Like Lazarus, many have been wrapped in garments of death and kept from the destiny God intended. This is a time when the Lord is crying out: "Women, come forth!" Many around the world are shaking off the old and being renewed. In past seasons, some women, like Aimee Semple McPherson and Maria Woodworth Etter, broke out of their cocoon and were successful in fulfilling their destinies. In this season of Kingdom restoration, I believe multitudes of women will answer God's call and pursue their destinies.

Today, the message of God's Kingdom is being heard with new understanding. God has been building His Church, but the focus has mainly been on church building. With the restoration of all five of the Ephesians 4:11 gifts (apostles, prophets, evangelists, pastors and teachers), the Church is being equipped to minister beyond the four walls of a building.

EMBRACING THE CALL

For many years as a pastor's wife, I sat on the pew, not really seeing myself as a minister. I taught Sunday School and led prayer meetings and the women's ministry, yet I did not really embrace the call to the ministry that I had received at the age of 16.

I heard the Lord call me to "full-time ministry" at a revival meeting when I was a teenager. Coming from a denominational background where women were not to speak in the church, I felt I should pursue being a missionary. To have ready access to the mission field, I became a nurse. But I was thrown off course again when I got married, became a pastor's wife and rationalized in my heart that I was fulfilling my call to ministry. I would watch my husband prepare sermons and think, *I am so glad that he is speaking and not me.* I lived in bondage to intimidation. I thought, *I could never do it as well as he could. I don't have anything to say. And preach? Oh my, I could never do that!* That cocoon of fear, inferiority and intimidation held me for a long time. *You can't, you can't, you can't!* rang in my ears for many years. Satan knows our weak spots and works to keep us bound! Even though I was glad Jim was doing all the preaching, deep in my heart I was not fulfilled and longed to be more useful to the Lord. The call of God I embraced at 16 was working in me. The mandate Christ gave was speaking to me: "You *can* go, you *can* have dominion, you *can* fill the earth with My word and you *can* walk in My covenant and build My Kingdom."

Then God began to change the season in my life. Barbara Wentroble, a prophet, joined our church, and the word of the Lord began to bring new understanding to me. She prophesied:

"God wants to use your mouth." Another prophet, Cindy Jacobs, prophesied to me: "You will preach." The first time she said it, I thought her tongue just slipped. But then she repeated it: "You will preach." After the third time she said it I began shaking under the power of God and was very amazed. It was several years before this word began to mature in my life. The Lord puts His prophetic word in us as a seed. We must water, cultivate, believe and act on that word for it to grow. After I received these words, doors began to open and invitations came for me to speak. Little by little, God began to send me out and develop my call.

GOD'S TIMETABLE

In February 2002, just before I turned 60, I was ordained to the ministry. Barbara Yoder's prophetic word to me on that day still rings in my ear: "You shall skip as a calf let out of the stall and you will run as a royal steed to the nations." Many years after receiving the call to the mission field, I boarded a plane for India, the first of many trips to the nations.

God has a timetable for our lives, but many times we think we have missed it or we can't do it. Fear, intimidation, discouragement and the words "you can't" hold us captive and immobile. God is saying: "You can, and you will!" He is removing the cultural burkas, the cocoons that have held us captive. His word is working in us to produce faith!

Apostolic women are being set free to be who they are in Christ. They reflect the heart of Deborah. They are humble, yet bold. They have a heart of submission, yet are not afraid to let their gifts make room for them. They refuse to usurp authority, yet boldly move in the authority of God's Word. They know their God and His calling and move out to do Kingdom exploits.

WINGS TO FLY

One thing they told us at the butterfly farm is that when the butterfly emerges, it sits in the sunlight, not moving for several hours. This allows the heat to dry its wings and give its heart time to pump blood into the wings to expand them to their full size. What a beautiful analogy of what God is doing for women. As we sit in the Son's presence, He is forming our wings so we can fly. His heart is pumping His love, His word and His life into us to mature us, so that we will reach our full stature in Him and fulfill His destiny for our lives. It doesn't matter what age we are. It only matters who we are in the Kingdom and what God's specific call and destiny is for our life. It's never too late to answer God's call!

CHAPTER 7

MANTLED WITH AUTHORITY

Barbara J. Yoder

What are you wearing? Women apostles and apostolic women are to be mantled with authority. Our mantle carries weight, power, reputation and authority. It is ample for our mandate. It is a glory from God that covers us. We are not to look wimpy, scared, indecisive, powerless or without reputation. We have been clothed supernaturally by God with the mantle of apostolic empowerment. We have been given influence and power sufficient to germinate and bring to birth seeds of destiny.

Through my hotel window I can see mountains cloaked with trees—trees that cause the mountains to express themselves in a unique way. These mountains are not like the looming masses of jutting rocks found in the Colorado Rockies. They are softer, rounder and less elevated, lacking that cold, barren boldness that pierces through whatever is in its way. The flowing branches of the fir trees mantling their surface seem to sing a calming yet strengthening song. They call out to me. I am drawn to them. I feel safe. These mountains look like my friends.

These characteristics differentiate them from the sense of raw power I feel when viewing the treeless Rockies. Those mountains are fearsome and overpowering, towering boldly above everything that surrounds them. They speak a different message. I feel a surge of energy rushing through me and courage seeping down into every part of my being. Suddenly, I feel bold and risky. Desire and confidence to break through overtake me. As I look at them something inside of me says, "Just do it! Nothing stands in your way or holds you back." I feel empowered, courageous and daring. Both mountain ranges have a message. Each has a different message that is formed by their structure and covering.

So it is with us. Apostles and apostolic women have authority. Our authority is in the mantle we wear. We look, feel and act differently. We are different. The difference is that we are clothed with a supernatural covering that causes others to perceive us in a unique way. We are mantled. How we are mantled makes all the difference in how we are perceived and in what we can accomplish. Let's consider mantles presented in Scripture.

MANTLES AND WHAT THEY REPRESENT

When Elijah identified his successor, he took his mantle, the mantle of a prophet, and threw it on Elisha (see 1 Kings 19). It was a cloak that represented Elijah's identity as well as what he was imparting to Elisha. What was Elijah doing? He was carrying out a prophetic action that declared to heaven and earth how Elisha was going to be perceived in days ahead. We know there was power in that mantle because Elisha, following Elijah's death, took that mantle and struck the waters of the Jordan River with it, and the waters parted. Now that's power!

Biblically, a mantle was a loose, sleeveless garment that was worn over other clothes. It represented something. Leaders dressed for their office and were identified by what they wore. Priests wore designated clothing as commanded by Levitical law. Kings dressed for their position, as did queens. Military people were distinguished by what they wore. Their dress spoke of their mantles; it represented their identity and authority.

Webster's Dictionary defines a mantle as a symbol of preeminence or authority.[1] The Hebrew word for mantle is *'addereth*.[2] The 'addereth was a robe (or garment), glory or something ample that one wore. I love that word "ample." How significant! The mantle Elijah wore was ample for the task. Furthermore, the mantle was a type of glory that Elijah, and later Elisha, wore. The apostle Peter spoke about the spirit of glory resting upon us (see 1 Pet. 4:14). One of the words for glory is weighty.[3] Glory is in the mantle and therefore adds weight to who we are and what we do. It represents the influence that we have. It is also our reputation. Something about us is recognized by others and identified as our reputation.[4] We say, "your reputation precedes you" (of course, it can be good or bad).

The feminine form of 'addereth is *'addiyr*.[5] This second word is translated as wide or large and powerful. It is also translated as excellent, famous, gallant, glorious, goodly, lordly, mighty, noble, principal or worthy. There is something communicated through a mantle that is powerful.

WHAT IS AUTHORITY?

Authority is a compelling concept in the New Testament.[6] It is translated as power in some passages. However, it is not power in the typical sense of the word. Power is strength, might and ability. Authority is different. It is the delegated, and therefore legal, right to be and do something. For example, a policeman as an ordinary citizen has no power to stop traffic. However, when he is in uniform, on duty, as a delegated official of the city law enforcement agency, he may stand in the street and direct traffic. Citizens obey him because they know who he is and what he has been given the authority to do. They respond to the office given him. He has delegated power from the city rulers to control traffic. Simply said, authority is the right to do something. That right comes from the official in control of the right that is given.

Furthermore, authority is privilege, capacity, competency, freedom or mastery. It is also translated as liberty, power, right and strength. Authority is power in conjunction with who the person is, not what the person does. Through wisdom, experience, knowledge, skill and mastery, individuals have authority. They have power or influence with people. People respect them because of who they are. When we speak of someone as being an authority in a subject area, it means they have mastered that area. First, the authority one is mantled with comes from whom that person is related to and who has delegated it to them. As God's delegates, we have been given His authority. Second, authority is acquired over time because of the breadth and depth of a person's wisdom, knowledge and experience.

One mentor in my life has been Patricia Beall Gruits. She is founder and president of Rhema International, an international medical mission and Bible school in Haiti.[7] She was mentored by her mother, Myrtle D. Beall, founder of Bethesda Missionary Temple in Detroit, Michigan. Although she does not call herself an apostle, she is one. She is a woman of authority. Why? Because her wisdom, knowledge, experience, integrity of character and relationship with God command attention. She does not have to yell or jump up and down. Her words are those of someone in authority. When she speaks, people listen. They stand to attention. She has authority because of who she is as well as what she has achieved. We should want to have both.

WHAT WE HAVE BEEN DELEGATED

God has given to all of us several things through authority. One is the authority to fully become the apostolic women He has called us to be. John 1:12 says that He has given us authority to become full-fledged family members with rights of inheritance. That's what sons are. Luke 10:19 says He has given us "authority to trample on serpents and scorpions, and over all the power of the enemy." In Luke 19:11-27, God delegates authority to us according to our faithfulness to carry out each task He gives us, beginning with the smallest. The level of our authority there is linked with our faithfulness to do what He has given us to do. One task completed qualifies us for the next level of authority.

Sometimes people want positions of authority when they have never demonstrated success in the position they currently hold. Furthermore, they may fail to meet the character qualifications necessary for the position, and they may have never been given the authority by God to stand in that place.

Believers will find their authority and their apostolic mandate in Genesis 1:28, Matthew 28 and Acts 1:8. Jesus gave us authority. Consider Matthew 28:18-20. Jesus said: "'All authority [legal right by My Father, God] has been given to Me *in heaven and on earth. Go therefore* and *make disciples* of all the nations, *baptizing them* in the name of the Father and of the Son and of the Holy Spirit, *teaching them* to observe all things that I have commanded you; and lo, I am with you always, even to the end of the age.' Amen" (emphasis added).

"Amen" means, *so be it*! Let's start to let it be on earth as it is in heaven! We have been mantled with authority as believers to do these things. Get this in your spirit. God has told us what to do. Furthermore, He has given us the authority needed to get the job done. If that isn't enough, consider the last thing Jesus told us in Acts 1:8. He said that He would give us a different kind of power to break through every hindrance blocking us from our legal position and releasing our legal authority. "You shall receive power when the Holy Spirit has come upon you; and you shall be witnesses to Me in Jerusalem, in all Judea and Samaria, and to the end of the earth." Here the word "power" means strength to break through and enabling power to get the job done. The Greek word is dunamis—the same word discussed in chapter 3.

MANTLES DEFINE IDENTITY

The second aspect of authority arises out of the specific identity God has given to each of us. Every believer, male and female, is mantled with apostolic authority to go forth, be and do. However, there is a specific assignment that identifies each of us and determines how our apostolic authority will be expressed. For example, Elijah's power and authority were unique to and inherent in the mantle assigned to him.

On December 29, 2002, Chuck Pierce declared that 2003 would be a year of mantles and miracles for the Church. What did that mean? To me it meant that we were to pick up and put on the mantle that God had assigned to us, and that miracles were in the mantle. Our mantle is our assignment from God with corresponding authority to fulfill it. To put on the mantle requires a miracle. First, we have to identify the mantle. Second, we have to put it on. If we cannot see it, we cannot put it on. If we don't put it on, we won't walk in it. If we do not walk in it, what has been destined by God to be released through us into the earth realm will never happen. Satan does not want any of us to put on our mantles and he will oppose us in any way he can. It requires us to break through. Look at the life of David. It took years for him to put on the clothes of a king. There was a war over his mantle, and there is a war over our mantle.

Favor Mantle

There are several different types of mantles. One I refer to as a Favor Mantle. Joseph had a Favor Mantle. This mantle was a coat of many colors, which represented the favor he had with his father. In fact, Joseph, though he was not the firstborn, received the double portion inheritance of the firstborn because he was so favored by his father. This mantle also represented the call that was on his life. He was a dreamer with a prophetic gift. But there was a war over his favor—his gift that would release his inheritance. His brothers stole his coat and ripped it up. His mantle got him into trouble with his brothers.

Years later, Joseph's mantle also got him out of trouble. He interpreted Pharaoh's dream and was released from prison. There are miracles in the mantle. Pharaoh gave Joseph new clothes—a new identity that represented the mantle he was to wear as ruler over Pharaoh's house (see Gen. 41:40). Our mantle will bring us into conflict, but we must keep exercising the gift in the mantle because it will eventually get us out of trouble.

Take note of Joseph's behavior prior to his appearance before Pharaoh. He shaved and changed his clothes. He went before Pharaoh not as a victim or captive, but as a freed man, sent forth by God to minister (see Gen. 40:14). We, as women, need to change our "clothes" so we can approach our pharaohs as freed ones, not as victims or captives.

Office Mantle

A second kind of mantle is an Office Mantle. In Ephesians 4:11, Paul identifies five different governmental offices or gifts. Those gifts are types of mantles, which carry corresponding abilities and miracles. The mantles of both the apostle and prophet carry revelation (see Eph. 3:5), signs and wonders (see 2 Cor. 12:12) and much more.

Evangelists' mantles carry the good news of the Gospel. Teachers' mantles put meat on the bones through the careful exposition of truth. Pastors' mantles shepherd the sheep with great love, care and concern. There is much more to each of these mantles.[8] They are full of gifts and miracles needed to fully release the ministry so that the Church is equipped, brought to maturity and comes into the unity of the faith (see Eph. 4:12-16). The mantles are full of apostolic authority.

Elijah wore an Office Mantle—that of the prophet. It identified who he was and, therefore, what he was to do. It was that same mantle that he threw on Elisha. The transfer of the mantle communicated to Elisha his identity and what his life focus was to be from that point forward.

Attitude Mantle

Scripture alludes to Attitude Mantles. Isaiah 61:4 speaks about putting on the garment of praise for the spirit of heaviness. What we wear will bring us into victory or defeat. Apostolic women give up the Attitude Mantles of depression, oppression, hopelessness and insecurity because they know those mantles will bring them into defeat. Instead, they wear mantles of expectation, faith, trust, hope, confidence and praise. It brings them corresponding results. Mantles evoke responses in others because we reap what we sow (see Gal. 5).

Humility Mantle

I love the book Peter Wagner wrote about humility.[9] It is a great, yet simple book. He refers to the verse in 1 Peter 5:5 that says, "Be clothed with humility, for God resists the proud, but gives grace to the humble." Peter describes humility as clothing. Whatever we wear must have the threads of humility weaved into its tapestry. Humility will release great grace to us. Grace is not only unmerited favor, but also the supernatural ability to walk in what God has called us to walk in. Pride will force others to resist us. They resist the assignment we are trying to carry out in the mantle we wear. Why? Because there is pride over what we are "wearing." Humility is the grace to submit. True apostles have great humility because they understand the power of submission. In submission, there is great authority.

Purity Mantle

God longs to pass out new mantles. In Zechariah 3:1-5, Joshua, the high priest, was completely redressed. Why? Filthy garments. He needed to be clean. There is a mantle of purity that apostolic people are to wear in order to keep their position and walk in great authority. The gift can get us in the door, but our character will keep us there. Joshua was clothed with filthy garments. But he stood up and appeared before the Lord anyway. God noticed his courage and humility. He then said in verse 4: "Take away the filthy garments from him. . . . I will clothe you with rich robes."

Royal Mantle

Royal Mantles will get us into the king's house. When Esther got ready to go before the king, she changed her clothes (see Esther 5:1-2). She put on her royal robes and stood in the inner court where the king was. As a result, the king noticed her and she found great favor in his sight. He then opened his heart to her to give her what she wished. Her clothes (mantle) caused her to be perceived in a way that she would not have been had she not changed her clothes.

Honor Mantle

In Esther 6:8-11, King Ahasuerus asked Haman how he should honor someone who he wanted to bring into his court. Haman told the king he should dress the one chosen with the king's royal robes and royal crest and that he should let that person ride on the royal steed. So when the time came, the king honored Mordecai by redressing him and putting him on the royal steed. This was an Honor Mantle. Mordecai had honored the king by forewarning him about a plot against his life (see Esther 6:2). As a result, he obtained favor. That favor brought Mordecai into great honor.

Mothering Mantle

The female side of the apostolic is a Mothering Mantle. This can mean being the mother of natural or spiritual children, or being the leader of a church, a nation or an organization. Mary was an "at-home" mother. Her primary job was to raise Jesus. The apostolic mantle on women includes those who have chosen to stay home and raise their children. An apostolic mother is one who proactively raises children according to their destiny and call. She helps identify and guide her children into the call of God on their lives. The Mothering Mantle operates to raise children with the essential education, character training and opportunities needed to prepare them to step into their destiny when the time comes. It also may require her to go to war over the fulfillment of her children's destiny.

An apostolic mother is discerning and aggressive when it comes to dealing with the enemy's tactics over her children. This was true for Mary and Joseph. The enemy tried to destroy Jesus' destiny by killing Him. The enemy also tries to destroy the lives and the destiny of our children. Whether or not we are at home, we, as apostolic mothers, need to rise up and protect the call and destiny of God on our children. It is a tremendous responsibility to take a child from birth and mold him or her into an adult, prepared to step into the full will of God. What great honor and privilege there is in raising godly children. What would happen if every believing Christian parent would begin to fully embrace this aspect of the apostolic call? "Behold, children are a heritage from the Lord, The fruit of the womb is a reward. Like arrows in the hand of a warrior, so are the children of one's youth. Happy is the man or woman who has his quiver full of them; they shall not be ashamed, but shall speak with their enemies in the gate" (Ps. 127:4-5).

Priestly Mantle

The last mantle I am going to mention is the Priestly Mantle. Exodus 40:12-16 outlines the special clothes the high priests were to wear during their service in the temple. This illustrates an important understanding. While some mantles are to be worn all the time, others are to be put on only when we assume the position of that mantle. *Mantles define function.* For example, I am an apostle who has a defined sphere of authority. When I am outside of that sphere, I am simply Barbara Yoder, daughter, sister, mother or friend. I am not apostle or prophet. When I step into my assignment from God, I put on the mantle associated with my assignment. At that point, what I do comes from the very presence and power of God connected with my assignment. It should be perceived differently than when I am hanging out with friends. My mantle defines my function. I am Barbara Yoder, whose mantle is that of an apostle and prophet. My mantle defines the position I am to assume and the functions I am to perform.

This is a day when God wants to give us authority and power corresponding to the mantle with which He has clothed us. We are in a time of great change. We must put on new clothes. In 1 Kings 11:29, when a "certain prophet" went before the king, he first had to put on the right clothes. There are places we are destined to step into that will require us to put on new clothes or clean up the ones we wear. New mantles are falling on individuals in the Church in this hour. How we position and conduct ourselves will determine whether we receive these new mantles and are able to keep them.

DISQUALIFIED FOR THE MANTLE

Elisha, the servant of Elijah, received the mantle passed onto him. He was faithful and served Elijah with impeccable character and abandonment. The mantle was physically and spiritually passed on to him (see 2 Kings 2). However, Elisha was not able to throw the prophet's mantle on his servant, Gehazi, even though Gehazi was the next in line to receive it (see 2 Kings 5). Gehazi disqualified himself. He was covetous (see v. 20) and a liar (see vv. 22,25). He deceived Naaman to get the goods that Naaman had wanted to give to Elisha and then lied to Elisha about the incident. A curse came upon him instead. He forfeited his mantle.

The enemy wants to keep all of us from receiving the mantle God has for us. Conceivably, one weapon he is using is disrespect, which has been so sown into the American youth culture that it may disqualify the next generation from receiving its mantle. Second Timothy 3:1-9 spells out many things that will disqualify us from receiving mantles of authority. Paul goes on to say that those who follow his doctrine will be made complete and thoroughly equipped for every good work (see 2 Tim. 3:10-17). Honoring others releases favor to us. Favor will result in mantles being released to us.

A NEW DAY

Women, this is not the day you are to remain hidden in obscurity—hidden in closets, hidden behind others, or hidden in an identity that God never intended for you. This is a new day. This is a day when you are to arise, mantled with great authority. You are to know the specific identity that is in the mantle you wear. You are to know who God is and understand the authority and power He has covered you with to become all that you are destined to be. Awaken the seeds of destiny and begin to sow them into all the earth. Let great faith arise, for this is the day when the reaper is going to begin to overtake the sower. Put on your robe of authority, power, influence, position and glory. Let the reputation of your authority be known far and wide. The glory of the Lord is arising over you. So arise and begin to shine. Put on your new clothes and dazzle the world. Women apostles and apostolic women, this is your day!

A NEW SEASON

Jane Hansen

I believe there has been a corporate calling forth and a worldwide awakening in the lives of women in a unique and unprecedented way. God is indeed up to something in women's lives. This awakening is unprecedented because never, in all of history, has a move quite like this occurred among women. As you look back through history, you can see that God has always used women, but it has been primarily in singular ways. But in these last days, He is revealing the significant role women will play in His end-time purposes in the earth.

A SHIFT IN THE SPIRIT

A shift has taken place in the spirit realm, and today, we find ourselves in a different season. The change occurred before September 11, 2001, and many in the Church were aware of that shift. However, now the world is aware as well. We have entered a different season nationally, politically and spiritually.

Habakkuk 1:2-4 reads like our response to today's newspaper: "O Lord, how long shall I cry, and You will not hear? Even cry out to You, 'Violence!' and You will not save. Why do You show me iniquity, And cause me to see trouble? For plundering and violence are before me; There is strife, and contention arises. Therefore the law is powerless, And justice never goes forth. For the wicked surround the righteous; therefore perverse judgment proceeds."

Look anywhere in the world on any given day and you will see violence, trouble, plundering, strife and contention. Indeed, the law seems powerless to bring the unrighteous to justice. But the Lord responds to the prophet, and He would respond to us as well: "Look among the nations and watch—Be utterly astounded! For I will work a work in your days which you would not believe, though it were told you" (Hab. 1:5).

As believers, we are keenly aware that the war on terrorism, this first war of the 21st century, is not just about terrorists. The real enemy, the real conflict, is not what is seen, but what is unseen. Daily we hear updates regarding terrorism. In September 2001, President Bush stated in a news broadcast that we cannot fight this war the way we have fought wars in the past. That is a true statement. This war will be fought on many different levels, but the central issue is spiritual. It is not as much about rights, or land, or territory, or even people, as it is about this central question: Who is the Most High God? Today we are at war with a spiritual enemy that has set himself against God Almighty. Whose throne will ultimately be established in the holy city of Jerusalem?

THE GARMENT OF ISLAM

In 1991, the Lord spoke prophetically to the ministry of Women's Aglow, an international women's organization in 151 nations in the world, saying *"it takes only one thread to unravel a garment, and even as you have seen the garment of communism unravel in this hour, I will give into your hands a thread that will begin to unravel the garment of Islam."* When I think of "the garment of Islam," I think of the burka, a garment worn by many Muslim women covering them from head to foot. It is physically, and in a spiritual sense, like a shroud. *Time* magazine called it "a body bag for the living."[1] God began to "unravel" that shroud by showing the world, in a very powerful way, the condition imposed upon women by a system.

Islam is more than a religion; it is a system that is woven into the very fabric of Muslim societies. It is a religious, political, economic, social, judicial, societal, and psychological system that keeps women bound as inferior beings. The enemy of mankind,

Satan, hates women and he is not above using religion to keep women bound from their god-Given purpose. I believe his wrath, his hatred, and his violence have been poured out against women down through the ages because he has an understanding of why God called the woman in the first place. He has come against women in a very clear, concise, focused and hateful way, because he knows that if women come into the full understanding of why God called them originally, he will no longer remain safe.

"I WILL GIVE YOU ISLAM"

Doesn't it seem that women would be unlikely deliverers for those caught in a system that has brought such oppression to the female gender? Yet God has raised up deliverers throughout history that were just as unlikely, such as Moses, Esther, and even Mary. And so, He is again today speaking to an unlikely group—a group of women. He is giving into their hands a thread that will begin to unravel the greatest antichrist spirit in the earth today. He will give us Islam if we will take it.

FOR SUCH A TIME AS THIS

You will recall that God raised up Esther to be queen and that it was she who exposed the plan of Haman to annihilate the Jewish people. Esther saved her people from destruction. According to Esther 3:1, Haman was a descendant of King Agag, leader of the Amalekites. They were the first tribe to attack the Israelites as they entered the Promised Land, and they remained bitter enemies (see Exod. 17:8-16). Because the Amalekites were, in effect, interfering with His plan through the nation of Israel, God declared His purpose for them—destruction (see 1 Sam. 15:2-3). King Saul disobeyed the command of the Lord to destroy the

Amalekites king (see 1 Sam. 8), and in so doing allowed the spirit of annihilation against the Jewish people to continue down through the centuries, until we see it once again functioning through Haman in the book of Esther. That spirit did not end with Haman's death on the gallows, but re-emerged through Hitler and his "final solution" to the "Jewish problem."

Today, I lead a ministry of Esthers called to stand in the gap for the people of Israel against the spirit of Haman, against the enemy's attempts to annihilate God's people, a plan that has persisted through the years. It is a ministry "for such a time as this" (see Esther 4:14). The meaning of "for such a time as this" is now becoming clear. Ordinary women are being called to expose the modern-day enemy of God's people. I believe one of the manifestations of the Haman spirit is through the system of Islam, which views Jews as well as Christians as infidels. The call is to love the Muslim people, but expose the system of Islam. How like God to prepare a ministry of "ordinary women," just as He did for Esther, to stand in the gap so that His purposes may come forth through His people—both Jew and Gentile. So you can see that God is doing a new thing!

WALKING IN THE LAND

In May 2002, I journeyed to Israel with 255 women. Many major ministries had cancelled trips to Israel because of the volatile conditions. The United States had issued travel advisory warnings. Tourism was down by 97 percent, hotels and restaurants were closing; the streets literally were desolate. As we walked the streets, prayed, made proclamations and met the Israeli people face-to-face, they were astounded that a group of women would come to Israel at a time when the Church seemed to be pulling back. I was reminded of the Scripture in Judges 5:6 that states, "The highways were deserted, and the travelers walked along the byways. Village life ceased, it ceased in Israel, until I, Deborah, arose, arose a mother in Israel."

WOMEN, ARISE!

Perhaps you are wondering, "What does this have to do with me as a woman?" Everything! Women will play a significant role in the end-time purposes of God. One of the names of God is Jehovah-Jireh, the God who sees ahead and provides. He sees and prepares for the need, so that when the hour comes, He has already made provision for what is needed in that season. God has been preparing women for their role in bringing forth what is on His heart for the Church, and for Israel.

God has always used women. There have been the Deborahs, the Esthers, the Abigails, the Jochebeds and the Hannahs. These were women who, out of the essence of their womanhood, were cooperating with God in furthering His plan in the earth, sometimes without even realizing it. Let's look at two.

JOCHEBED AND HANNAH

The mother of Moses, Jochebed, was a woman of faith. When the edict came from Pharaoh to destroy all male Hebrew babies, her response sprang from the very essence of her womanhood—from her mother's heart. She must preserve the life of her son! So she hid him, and ultimately placed him in a basket among the reeds of the great Nile River (see Exod. 2:1-12). An act that appeared very ordinary and simple, and very typical of a woman, was the very thing God needed at that moment for His plan to move another step forward. For Moses' birth was God's way of setting in motion the deliverance of His people that He had been planning for nearly 400 years. So it would seem that the ongoing plan of God in the earth hinged on the response of a woman.

Hannah struggled with infertility. Barrenness for the women of that time was a source of terrible shame. Out of her pain and a deep longing to have a child, she grieved and wept before the Lord. She was a woman who just wanted a baby! But God was in the midst of Hannah's barrenness. He was again orchestrating something from heaven for the furtherance of His plan and purpose on Earth. You see, barrenness was not only the condition of Hannah, it was also the spiritual condition of God's people. The Bible says in 1 Samuel 3:1, "the word of the Lord was rare in those days."

God wanted someone who would have an ear to hear and a heart to follow and through whom He could bring forth His word in that hour. So God found a woman: a woman who, from the essence of her womanhood, would begin to cry out and plead with Him for a child. But there came a point when Hannah stepped out of her own need and into the purposes of God: "if you will indeed look on the affliction of Your maidservant and . . . give me a male child, then I will give him to the Lord all the days of his life" (1 Samuel 1:11). It was the moment God was waiting for; the words He wanted to hear. He had a willing vessel through whom He could birth one of the greatest prophets Israel would ever know (see Ps. 99:6; Jer. 15:1; Acts 3:24; Heb. 11:32). So God moved on Hannah's behalf. He was actually moving on His own behalf in order to bring forth the fullness of His plan in the earth. Once again, it would seem the ongoing plan of God hinged on the response of a woman.

And so it is with us. God is looking for women in this hour who are willing to step out of their own desires and needs into the purposes and plan of God. He is drawing us away from our self-seeking ways to become seekers of Him. As we embrace His destiny for us, we become participants in His ongoing plan in the earth.

WOMEN: A KEY TO RESTORING THE CHURCH

One of the reasons God has been awakening women in such a significant way is because of the crucial role they hold in His end-time plan. He has been healing, restoring and bringing us into an understanding of the purposes for which we were created, so that His plan for the Church can come forth. Ephesians 1:11 states: "[He] works all things after the counsel of His will." "All things" means *everything*. Everything God does, He does with the fulfillment of His plan in mind. Scripture tells us that the heavens will hold Jesus back until all things have been restored (see Acts 3:21). What is God restoring? It is the Church! We are told in Isaiah 60:2 that "darkness shall cover the earth, and deep darkness the people; but the Lord will arise over you, and His glory will be seen upon you." His light and glory are being manifested in us as He restores us to His original design.

IN THE BEGINNING

The reconciliation of men and women is a powerful truth because it is a foundational truth in the restoration of the Church. In Genesis 1:26-27, the Word says "'Let us make man in Our image, according to Our likeness'. . . . So God created man in His own image; in the image of God He created him; male and female He created them." God blessed them and told them to be fruitful, multiply, subdue the earth and take dominion over it (see Gen. 1:28). So, from the beginning, He told us what dominion would look like in the earth. It was male and female. He called them together, not separately. God's purpose is to bring forth a reconciled Church, one that is restored to His original design. For the Church to fulfill the destiny God has planned in the full expression of power and authority, this foundational truth must be understood and embraced by His people.

God's original intention was that His image be shared between men and women. In order for His image, His character and His likeness to be expressed on the earth in the fullest way, it must be seen, heard, felt and known through both men and women. God will yet bring forth the fullness of His image and glory in the earth as He reconciles men and women to His original design.

DIVIDE AND CONQUER

It wasn't happenstance that the enemy came to the woman first in the Garden. He had been present when God said that man's aloneness was not good and that He would make a helper suitable for him (see Gen. 2:18). Satan knew that in order to disrupt the whole plan of God, the best approach would be to attack the help God had sent. So he came to the woman first, seeking to bring division between the man and the woman, hence undermining God's plan.

Have you ever wondered why there is such violence and wrath poured out against women in so many cultures of the world? I believe we see the answer to this in Genesis 3. It was the woman who clearly exposed the enemy for who he really is—the deceiver. Following the fall of humanity, and in response to God's questions, she said, "The serpent deceived me, and I ate" (Gen 3:13). The Lord then turned to the Serpent and said, "I will put enmity between you and the woman, and between your seed and her Seed; He shall bruise your head, and you shall bruise His heel" (Gen 3:15). In a sense, God was saying: "Now forever and ever, Satan, down through the centuries, she will be used again and again to expose you and call you who you really are, the deceiver!"

The perfect fulfillment of this Scripture came with the birth of Jesus. But there is an ongoing fulfillment that continues to take place. From Eve onward, ordinary women like you and me—the Esthers, Jochebeds and Hannahs—have been used to expose the enemy. As women, we bring forth natural life. He has written into our very nature the ability and desire to give birth. As it is in the natural, so it is in the spiritual realm also. Often, it is a woman who will lay hold of the very will of heaven for her family, her loved ones and her community. She will then carry it in the womb of her spirit and bring to birth in the earth that which God purposed in heaven. She was created with a unique sensitivity to the needs of those around her and to the heart of God. As she is awakened to God and is turned from herself and her selfish needs, she becomes a very powerful tool in the hands of God—and an effective adversary of Satan.

WOMEN, YOU ARE SATAN'S ENEMY!

We often refer to Satan as our enemy, but in a very real way the exact opposite is true. *We* are *his* enemy. He has known this truth from the beginning, for God stated it directly to him in Genesis 3:15. Because of this fact, he has worked to silence women and render them useless and powerless. He has brought intimidation and fear. He has brought the shrouds, the burkas in the spirit realm, to keep women enclosed, unsure and afraid. He causes women to focus inwardly on personal needs and wants. God wants to free women from themselves and their preoccupation with self to become seekers of and for Him.

In the 1960s and 1970s, we saw the birth of the radical feminist movement. Its message was a militant, strident demand to be heard. In a sense, some of it involved the honest cry of women's hearts, but it came in the wrong spirit. Interestingly, it was in this same timeframe that God began to raise up a woman's movement called Aglow. It ran parallel to the feminists and showcased to the world what a Spirit-filled, Spirit-led woman of God looks like. It was preparation for women to come into their destiny in God. It was a forerunner to the kind of women's movements God is using in the earth today—women with appropriate brokenness, which leads to wholeness and restoration.

THE VIRTUOUS WOMAN

God created the woman to be a "help" to the man because his aloneness was not good (see Gen. 2:18). The word "help" means to surround and to protect, to succor and to bring aid to someone in difficulty or distress. We, as women, don't think of ourselves as a man's protector, but in the spirit realm, we are. Did you know that the word "virtuous" spoken of in Proverbs 31:10, is a *warring* word?[2] The virtuous woman is a warrior woman. She is strong, able, forceful and powerful; she is one who is willing to go to battle. In the Hebrew language, the word "virtuous" actually pictures her as one single woman coming with the strength of an army. It comes from a root word that means to labor and travail in order to bring forth life.[3] What an interesting combination. She is a warrior. She is a birther. She is like a dog with a bone! When she gets hold of God and what He is calling her to do, there is nothing that can stand against her.

The virtuous woman "girds herself with strength, and strengthens her arms. She perceives that her merchandise is good" (Proverbs 31:17-18). "She looks well to the ways of her household" (v. 27, KJV). The word "looks" in this Scripture is the same word that is used in Ezekiel to describe the watchman on the wall.[4] She not only watches over her family, she also speaks the word of the Lord that she sees. "She is not afraid of snow for her household, for all her household has been covered with scarlet" (v. 21, KJV). Snow or cold is often metaphoric in Scripture for sin or God's judgment against sin.[5] Thus, she is not afraid of God's judgment, for she has covered her household with the blood of Jesus. She has heard the plan and purpose of God for her husband and her children, and she will bring to birth God's destiny for them. She is tenacious. She is a birther and will carry His word in the womb of her spirit until it is time to press against that which impedes and holds back God's will. Not only will she act on her family's behalf, but also for those in her work place, in her church, in her city, in the government and in the world!

THE DESTINY OF THE CHURCH

God is coming to release us in a greater way to all that He purposed for us as women, and for men as well, in this final hour. No longer can we allow the enemy to continue his plan to strike at the core of our maleness and femaleness. No longer can we allow the enemy and the world to define who we are as women and men. No longer will we be fashioned by the world. We will allow God to bring us back to His original design: male and female together expressing His image in the earth. This is God's purpose for the Church, His plan from the beginning; it is the foundational structure God chose for His Church. Because of that, the enemy will fight hardest against reconciliation between the genders.

The Church is beginning to walk in this kind of reconciliation, but we are not yet to the place He is leading us. We will see a merging of anointing between men and women that will lead us into our destiny together. This unprecedented move of God among women and, in the last number of years, among men through Promise Keepers, is not about creating a separate men's organization or a separate women's organization; it is about bringing us into wholeness and health so that we can begin to move into the fullness of what God planned from the beginning.

We have yet to see the Church display the strength, anointing and authority that God intended. However, a shift has occurred. We are in a different season: nationally, politically and spiritually. The pace is accelerating, and I believe that God is uniting us in a way that scares the enemy to death. We are casting off intimidation and fear. All the things that have kept us apart are being healed and restored so that we will be one, even as Jesus prayed, male and female, Jew and Gentile. God's glory will be seen in His people such as we have not yet known.

After God spoke His plan into being in the first three chapters of Genesis, He sat down and rested. He rested because He knew He had set in place His perfect plan. Nothing could abort, hinder or stop that plan from coming to fruition—not sin, not time, not flesh, not the devil. He is inviting us to that same posture of rest. To know and trust that what He has set in place, He *will* accomplish!

A CALL TO WOMEN

In this critical hour, the Lord is calling women to come before the King, just as Esther did, willing to be used "for such a time as this." When the king extended his scepter to her, as she stepped forward to touch it, she stepped into a new anointing and a new authority. I believe God is calling us, His women, to step into the fullness of our destiny with a new anointing and a new authority. Will you respond to the King?

CHAPTER 9

DEBORAHS, AWAKE!

Barbara J. Yoder

You may say you are just an ordinary woman. You are neither an apostle nor apostolic in nature. You want a nice, quiet, little life with good little children, a good school and a nice church that makes you feel good when you go on Sunday. You may also want to go back to life the way it was before September 11, 2001. But I say to you that September 11, 2001, ushered in a whole new reality. Whether we asked for it or not, whether we want it or not, it is here. Life is not the same. This new reality may exist for some time, perhaps the rest of our lives. Am I a pessimist? *No*! I have never been so charged up and optimistic. I am simply saying that we are in a "new world" in America. We are learning, whether we want to or not, the way many in the rest of the world live.

This is a new day. A shift has taken place. Peter Wagner declared that September 11 marked the beginning of the emergence of the New Apostolic Reformation Church. It is the second coming of the Church, the latter day Church, which will be greater than the former (see Hag. 2:9). To ignore what is happening is to fail to interpret the times. We can either live out life the rest of our days frustrated, trying to get back to the way our lives were before, or we can see what is and move into it with confidence and great joy. *This is the day that the Lord has made,* and I will (choose to) be glad and rejoice in it (see Ps. 118:24).

DELIVERED INTO A NEW PLACE

Though the atmosphere is agitated and disturbing, these are days of great potential. God is trying to shift us into the new; a place where how we understand and see things is congruent with the times in which we live. He is pouring out new wine and only new wineskins will be able to hold it.

In 2002, I experienced a time of darkness for almost six weeks. I did not understand what was happening. My husband had died three years prior to this time; yet what I was experiencing was not grief. This was different. In fact, it was quite disconcerting and I didn't know how to interpret it. My only option was to seek the Lord and search His Word. During that time, the Lord spoke to my heart, "I have turned out the lights in the old place so you can no longer go back there." Suddenly, I understood. God was forcing me into the new paradigm. I must be who He called me to be: an apostle. I could either resist the new place and die, or I could embrace His words and advance. I did not know how to be an apostle, nor did I want a title. Yet I had to break through the barrier and begin to say, *I am an apostle of God*. Why? Because it identified what I must do and how I should position myself in days ahead.

THE AWAKENING OF DEBORAH, WOMAN APOSTLE

Deep within my spirit, it was as if I could hear, "Deborah, Awake!" In Scripture, Deborah was the national leader of Israel. Today, we would call her an apostle, even though she was called a prophet at that time. Apostles were not identified as such in the Old Testament. In Judges 5:12, the song implores Deborah to *awake*. That word "awake" means "to open the eyes, literally to wake up; to lift yourself up; to stir yourself up."[1] The primitive root is to be made bare or naked.[2] In other words, who is the real you? What is the truth about your real identity? Only out of our true identity will we begin to see life as God wants us to see it. He is saying, "Open your eyes and see things as they really are." Remove the trappings and begin to look reality in the eye.

In that same verse, Barak was told to *arise*! But not Deborah. Deborah was told to *awake*. Perhaps this describes the day we live in. Women may not want to open their eyes. Why? If a woman sees, then she is responsible for what she sees. She would have to take action. It has not been comfortable for some women to step into the places and positions that God is inviting them to assume in this hour. To become an apostle or to be apostolic in nature is foreign to many women.

Deborah was an amazing woman. She was a female apostle, a mother, called to arise in the midst of great adversity and lead her people into freedom. She led the entire nation of Israel in a time of war. Before she arose, the environment was adversarial and hostile. They were under siege by other nations. People were on edge. Judges 5:6-7 says the land was so dangerous that the highways were deserted, travelers walked in hidden places so they didn't get killed and village life stopped—until Deborah arose as a mother in Israel. Because of what Deborah accomplished during her rule, the land was freed and had rest for 40 years.

Deborah became a leader in the war along with Barak. She not only ruled, but she went out against and overcame the enemy with Barak. The apostolic mind-set is one that is made for war. Apostles are like generals in the Armed Forces. When President George W. Bush announced what the United States would do regarding Iraq in March 2003, he explained that no leader had ever done this before in the history of the United States. This war was a new paradigm. President Bush was calling for an offensive war, not a defensive one. Regardless of one's position concerning the war, he was modeling for us in the natural realm what God wants His people to accomplish in the supernatural realm. God does not want His apostolic people to merely react to the attacks of the enemy. He wants us to take the offensive. An apostolic mindset is one that sets the boundaries before the enemy attacks.[3]

APOSTOLIC POSITIONING FOR BATTLE: OFFENSIVE, NOT DEFENSIVE

Apostolic positioning is offensive, not defensive. It takes action to stop the enemy before he can get a footing. It moves into a territory and penetrates hostile environments with the gospel and causes the kingdom of God to come into that place. We see that modeled again and again in Acts. In Acts 19, Paul invaded Ephesus with the gospel. It changed the city, the government, the economy and the ruling power. It removed that which brought death. It released life, liberty, destiny, prosperity and advancement. John 10:10 says that the enemy comes to steal, kill and destroy. But Jesus has come that we might have life—abundant, abounding, overflowing life.

What is war? War is conflict, combat, warfare, hostilities, fighting, arguments, confrontation, battles and military campaigns. We war over God's heart and purposes (His covenant promises) being fulfilled in our own lives, in the Church, in cities, in the nation and between nations. Paul said in 2 Corinthians 10:4 that "the weapons of our warfare are not carnal, but [they are] mighty through God to the pulling down of strongholds" *(KJV)*. The Greek word for warfare in this passage is *strateia*, which means military service.[4] The apostolic career is one of hardship and danger. It is derived from *strateuomai*, which means to serve in a military campaign, to execute the apostolate (with its arduous duties and functions) and to contend with carnal inclinations.[5] It means to go to war.

HAVING A MIND TO WAR

War is foreign in many respects for women. Traditionally, it has been seen as a man's place. Yet for the apostolic church, it is ordinary and commonplace, and it must be embraced if we are to obtain victory. Deborah awakened, called forth Barak to lead the nation into war, and then accompanied him because he would not go without her. Great victory was achieved. We must have a mentality to fight and to break through every barrier and hindrance.[6] Paul went into Ephesus and boldly preached the gospel in a hostile environment. The whole city was changed as a result.

War and breakthrough go together. We have to war to break through to the revelation necessary to advance. Daniel warred in order to break through in Daniel 10. He was warring with territorial powers. Revelation breaks through darkness with new light concerning God, His purposes, our place and our understanding of how we need to move forward. War begins with entering into worship to ascend into the very presence of God, because without Him, we will not get anywhere. It is His heart, His purposes, His direction and His orders that we want to embrace. Revelation 4:1 tells us to come up into heaven to see what God is saying and doing. Because the enemy does not want this to happen, there is conflict over entering into God's presence, before His throne, to meet with Him. Satan wants to keep us blind, deaf and dumb.

Many women war with mindsets of fear, ignorance, deception, stubbornness or insecurities that keep them from moving into that which God wants them to move into and obtain. They war with the past and how they have seen and done things that now have become a method, and with a way of life that is no longer relevant. Some war because of past failures, inadequacies and betrayals that threaten to hold them out of their rightful place and keep them from seeing both their destiny and the promises of God fulfilled.

SOME WARS WILL ONLY BE WON BY MALE-FEMALE TEAMWORK

Barak told Deborah he wouldn't go to war without her. Deborah was neither intimidated nor afraid of war. Why? It wasn't about keeping herself safe—she was freeing the covenant people of God. She had a holy mandate from God. She was a woman with a mission. Because of that, all of heaven fought with her and Barak to bring them into victory. Judges 5:4-5 implies that God was marching with them. It says, "Lord, when You went out from Seir, when You marched from the field of Edom, the earth trembled and the heavens poured, the clouds also poured water; the mountains gushed before the Lord, this Sinai, before the Lord God of Israel." Verse 13 also reiterates this: "The Lord came down for me against the mighty." Verse 20 says, "They fought from the heavens; the stars from their courses fought against Sisera. The torrent of Kishon swept them away, that ancient torrent, the torrent of Kishon. O my soul, march on in strength!"

Deborah's mission was not unanimously endorsed. The tribes of Reuben, Gilead, Dan and Asher ended up not going (see Judg. 5:15-17). Yet she did not let that stop her. Deborah understood a basic principle: leaders must lead. When leaders lead, people will arise and willingly follow them. Furthermore, the purpose of leading is to loosen locks. In Judges 5:2, the footnote in the margin of my Bible interprets "when leaders lead in Israel" as "when locks are loosed." Deborah was taking her place and leading. The people were then able to get into their assigned places because the locks that had held them out of their place were loosed. They were unlocked. The people were set free to be who they were and recover their covenantal inheritance.

ORDINARY WOMEN RELEASING VICTORY

Jael was an ordinary housewife, taking care of her tent. Nobody looked to her for great leadership. She was neither a general nor the head of a country. Yet she understood that when she found Sisera, the commander of the enemy's army, he had been delivered into her hands. A divine opportunity walked into her tent. She gave him milk, which some say was fermented, and therefore, intoxicating. When he fell asleep, she drove a peg into his temple, killing him. Jael, an unknown woman, knew when to set aside the mind of a housewife and enter into war on behalf of the covenant people of God. She played a significant role in Israel's victory (see Judg. 4:17-23).

APOSTOLIC GATHERING

Deborah was a gatherer. She gathered the nation together and rallied its forces around a vision, a purpose and a mission to be accomplished. Military leaders followed her. Ordinary housewives followed her. The whole nation followed her because she rose up and accepted the call of God to lead. The first statement in Judges 5:2 is about leaders leading. The next statement expresses how people will respond when leaders step to the plate; "people willingly offer themselves." They volunteer. People need to be moved to action. Great leaders, through passion, light a fire in followers. They will gather to the leader because something within them has been ignited and they want to participate in what is happening. Jesus, the apostle of our faith, ignited something in people and they followed Him. He gathered people to Himself.

PIONEERING

Deborah was a pioneer. Apostles are pioneering in nature. Pioneers lead us into new frontiers and break us through into new and uninhabited territories. They cut through uncharted lands and establish new settlements and initiatives. Pioneers make a way where there is no way. They are not afraid of wilderness territory. To them, it is a challenge to cut a new path so that others can follow, move into new territories and find new treasures. Pioneers initiate new works and new moves of God. Deborah pioneered; she broke through into a new place. She paved the way for Israel to enter into peace and obtain the spoils of war. We need women who are not afraid to cut new paths, to pioneer new works and to move into uncharted territory.

Aimee Semple McPherson was a pioneering apostle. In the early part of the 20th century, she founded the Foursquare International Denomination and built one of the most impressive architectural church structures in the United States. Multitudes came to Christ, were baptized in the Holy Spirit and were healed and delivered through her innovative and, at times, controversial ministry. I understand that one time she rode a motorcycle into the church and onto the platform. She knew how to get people's attention, and multitudes were redeemed so that their covenantal inheritance could be restored to them.

Isabella Baumfree, a black woman, was born into slavery around 1797. Because of her mother, she developed a deep and unwavering Christian faith that carried her through her entire life, including every trial she endured as a slave. Through her spiritual experiences and pioneering spirit, she renamed herself Sojourner Truth. She became a prominent abolitionist who also spoke on women's suffrage. Her most famous speech was "Ain't I a Woman?"

During the Civil War, she raised food and clothing contributions for the black regiments. In 1864, she met Abraham Lincoln at the White House. Amazingly, she spoke mostly to white audiences concerning religion, "Negro" rights, women's rights and temperance. Sojourner Truth was a pioneer, forging a new path. She was bold and broke through to new places and positions. She set a new course. Listen to her politically and religiously incorrect preaching (she was raised as a black slave on a

Dutch farm and originally spoke only Dutch, which is the reason for her speech being as it is):

> "Den dey talks 'bout dis ting in de head; what dis dey call it?" ("Intellect," whispered some one near.) "Dat's it, honey. What's dat got to do wid womin's rights or nigger's rights? If my cup won't hold but a pint, and yourn holds a quart, wouldn't ye be mean not to let me have my little half-measure full?" And she pointed her significant finger, and sent a keen glance at the minister who had made the argument. The cheering was long and loud.
>
> "Den dat little man in black dar, he say women can't have as much rights as men, 'cause Christ wan't a woman!' Whar did your Christ come from?" Rolling thunder couldn't have stilled that crowd, as did those deep, wonderful tones, as she stood there with out-stretched arms and eyes of fire. Raising her voice still louder, she repeated, "Whar did your Christ come from? From God and a woman! Man had nothin' to do wid Him." Oh, what a rebuke that was to that little man.
>
> Turning again to another objector, she took up the defense of Mother Eve. I can not follow her through it all. It was pointed, and witty, and solemn; eliciting at almost every sentence deafening applause; and she ended by asserting:
>
> "If de fust woman God ever made was strong enough to turn de world upside down all alone, dese women togedder (and she glanced her eye over the platform) ought to be able to turn it back, and get it right side up again! And now dey is asking to do it, de men better let 'em." Long-continued cheering greeted this. "Bleeged to ye for hearin' on me, and now ole Sojourner han't got nothin' more to say."[7]

DIRECT, SUSTAIN, MOTIVATE AND COMPLETE

Deborahs have an apostolic assignment to direct, sustain and motivate whatever they have initiated. Deborah governed and brought Israel into a new order. Apostolic people govern and order their spheres of assignment.[8] The apostles in the New Testament went into new areas, preached the gospel of the Kingdom and set things in order. They appointed elders and established foundational truth. Deborah dispensed judgments to the children of Israel, and then she ordered the battle by putting Barak in charge of deploying the troops. She governed the nation (her sphere of assignment) and set the nation in order (see Judg. 4:4-7). She motivated Barak and the people to act.

FACILITATE

Apostles are facilitators. They direct the flow of God's power and anointing. I had the privilege of speaking at a national conference in Brisbane, Australia. The night I was to speak, the Holy Spirit came in such a way that I could not preach. All I could do was facilitate, direct and govern the flow of the Holy Spirit for about 90 minutes. I never was able to go to my notes. I simply orchestrated what God wanted to do. This is one aspect of the apostolic. Apostles are not to do it all. They are to be facilitators who direct the flow of God's power and anointing. They are to identify the people and resources that need to be freed in order to move in the gifting and power that God has placed within them.

BUILD

Apostles are builders. The apostolic anointing builds people up. Zechariah 1:18-21 is a picture of this aspect and presents a vision that Zechariah had. His vision was that four powers came in to scatter Judah, Israel and Jerusalem. They so terrified the nation that the people could not lift up their heads. They were beaten down, depressed and hopeless. But builders (carpenters) came in, terrified, and dispelled the powers.

Think of what happens when a life is rebuilt *or* reconstructed. That which overcame a person in the past is no longer able to do so in the present because that person is completely different. They think and feel differently. A new foundation has been built in their life through the Word of God. Consider the ministry of Cleansing Stream Ministries, directed by Chris Hayward and born out of Dr. Jack Hayford's church, Church On The Way. That ministry is like a carpenter that rebuilds a life; the enemy has no place to terrify, discredit or defeat the person any longer. This is one type of apostolic building. Deborah rebuilt the nation first by empowering people and then by identifying and dispelling the invading force. The people stepped into place, overcame the enemy and took the spoils. This resulted in the nation coming into a 40-year period of rest. A woman led the nation to break through to its inheritance by building it up.

What builders raise up, lasts. It is critical that they build and impart spiritual wisdom and insight into the generations. Builders build bridges between people, generations, ministries, leaders, nations, businesses and governments. They connect disjointed parts through relationship and releasing vision. They gather and construct an inheritance for the next generation. They invest for the long-term results. They are not "flash-in-the-pan" minded. Builders see gifts and abilities in people and know how to release and put them together so that something is constructed that impacts people. They mobilize people and resources.

VISION DIRECTED RELATIONSHIPS

Deborah was vision-minded. She saw where the nation needed to go and set out to take it there. Apostles are also visionaries who desire to move things forward. They are not maintainers. They are movers and shakers. God is looking for women who are not stuck seeing things as they are, but will seek God and discover how things should be, and then move them there.

We need people who are both relational and visionary. So many groups get sidetracked and derailed because they focus primarily on relationship and fail to define relationship by vision. Consequently, nothing moves forward. Eventually these groups will either deteriorate into nonexistence or be taken over by maintainers and become stagnant. They will not move groups, cities and nations forward. We need apostolic visionaries to frame relationships so that we can move forward into the future and become all that God is challenging us to be. We are not called to form cliques that become so entrenched in relationship that no one can get in and no one can get out. Groups built on relationship alone can become stuck, like some women's clubs entrenched in tradition, and will go nowhere fast.

REFORMERS

Apostles are reformers. Reformers are lionhearted. Martin Luther King, Jr. was a reformer. Sojourner Truth was a reformer. Deborah reformed the nation. Hannah played a part in reforming Israel when she cried out to God for a son and birthed Samuel. The nation had fallen into degradation through Eli's failure to discipline his sons. Hannah initiated a reformation through a changing of the order. She birthed a new generation that followed the Lord (see 1 Sam. 1–3). Mary, the mother of Jesus, became supernaturally impregnated and birthed Jesus, the Messiah, who forever changed the world. Because of Christ, we now can take back the authority that Adam and Eve lost. We are on the verge of a reformation. God is looking for mothers who will reform their natural and spiritual children into shakers and movers who will change the world and create a Greater Awakening than the first one. Reformers see what is not working and ineffective, and then they begin to cry out for change.

FATHERS AND MOTHERS

Apostles are fathers and mothers. We need both. You cannot have a father without a mother. You cannot have children without both. The absence of one without the other creates dysfunction in a family. So it is in the Church. Many are asking, where are the fathers? We should also ask, where are the mothers? Where are those who will raise up and mentor the next generation? Where are those who will give away everything they have and know to empower those to whom the torch will be passed? I believe that the younger generation is crying out for mothers and fathers. There is a remnant of youth who is looking for, and will receive, what the fathers and mothers have to impart to them. Let's look for them and find them!

FINISHERS

Finally, apostles are finishers. Deborah got the job done. She finished what she began. She brought the nation into a time of peace. Apostolic leaders never give up. They endure every hardship. They persevere in the face of every adversity and persecution. David was like that. The *New King James Version* says that "David strengthened himself in the Lord" (1 Sam. 29:6). He recovered his faith and was able to seek and believe God for revelation on how to proceed. He then arose and did what God directed him to do (see 1 Sam. 30:7-9). Like David, apostolic people turn to God and encourage themselves in the Lord (see 1 Sam. 30:6). They find great strength in God to fulfill their assignments. They will see their projects through to fulfillment. No matter what rises up against them, they will break through every obstacle and hindrance.

What I am stating here is that we are to not only start well; we are to navigate every adversity so that we accomplish our God-given assignments. In his classes, Bobby Clinton admonished leaders not only to start, but to finish well.[9] He was speaking about character as well as vision. Some leaders do not fail to fulfill their life assignments because of sin; they fail to finish well because they lose their vision in and/or through a blind spot. They become discouraged, burn out and cannot see. They plateau, failing to move on to the next level.

True apostles will finish well. They rise above every temptation, overcome every adversity, break through every snare and leap over every wall to complete that which God has assigned them to accomplish. These apostles and apostolic women are those who have found a secret place in God. When hardship comes their way, they turn away from what they see and hear and turn to God. They have learned the lesson of abiding in the secret place:

> He who dwells in the secret place of the Most High shall abide under the shadow of the Almighty. I will say of the Lord, "He is my refuge and my fortress; My God, in Him I will trust." Surely He shall deliver you from the snare of the fowler and from the perilous pestilence. He shall cover you with His feathers, and under His wings you shall take refuge; His truth shall be your shield and buckler . . .
>
> Because you have made the Lord, who is my refuge, even the Most High, your dwelling place, no evil shall befall you, nor shall any plague come near your dwelling; for He shall give His angels charge over you, to keep you in all your ways. In their hands they shall bear you up,

lest you dash your foot against a stone. You shall tread upon the lion and the cobra, the young lion and the serpent you shall trample underfoot.

Because he has set his love upon Me, therefore I will deliver him; I will set him on high, because he has known My name. He shall call upon Me, and I will answer him; I will be with him in trouble; I will deliver him and honor him. With long life I will satisfy him, and show him My salvation (Psalm 91:1-4,9-16).

God is looking for a Deborah company to awake and take its place. Deborah, where are you? Awake, open your eyes and see the call of God before you. People and nations are crying out for you; for deliverers, builders, reformers, mentors and mothers; for people who will come and equip them for the task ahead. Who will awake, overcome the adversary and rebuild nations? Who will rebuild homes, corporations, governments, schools, the lives of youth and the Church?

DEBORAHS, WE NEED YOU! AWAKE!

Deborahs, the world needs you along with the fathers. Awake and take your place! Bring us forth into the new. We are looking and waiting for you. Awaken the passion and purpose within us. Focus us for the mission ahead. Speak to us in such a way as to ignite our hearts with strength and desire to overcome every adversity. Embolden us to take back that which has been stolen from us. Call us forth and we will follow. And when we follow, the Lord and the hosts of heaven will fight with us as we join with you to get back that which has been stolen by the enemy. Deborah stands as the righteous example before us. Deborah, our leader, our mother in Israel, our deliverer and judge, our advocate with the Father through Christ Jesus; Deborah, *Awake!*

CHAPTER 10

THE EMERGING GENERATION

Barbara J. Yoder

Something is shifting in this season. Everywhere I go, I see so many in their late teens and twenties wanting to connect with my generation. I have never seen anything like it. They are not ordinary. They are the Deborahs and Esthers who will change the world. This group is not like Gehazi. They have the spirit of Elisha. They want to serve the older generation so they can glean everything essential to fulfill God's plan for their life. They want to hang out to talk and talk and talk so that they can glean wisdom, counsel and experience to move into the next place. They are searching for God and spiritual reality. They are looking for relationship that touches their depths.

REFORMATION FOR REVOLUTION

A few years ago, the Lord spoke to me that the generation in their late teens and twenties would be part of a reformation that would precipitate a revolution in the church world. I kept hearing the words: "reformation for revolution." There is a revolutionary seed in that generation. *What would happen if my generation would actively recognize and embrace them?*

This younger generation is not thinking small. I have met young men and women who are preparing now to do what is in their heart. They plan to become not just senators or representatives, but Speakers of the House, Senate Majority Leaders and Secretaries of the Treasury. They see beyond the present and into the future of what they can be!

RELIGIOUSLY INCORRECT

The upcoming generation is not religiously correct. They are like my granddaughter, Tarrah, who, when asked by an interviewer for a mission trip who she was, boldly answered, "I am called to be an apostle." No hesitation, no awkward shyness; just bold words blurting out answers to questions. She never thought to be careful about her words or worry that someone might disagree or think she was presumptuous. Tarrah knows who she is and what she wants to do. Furthermore, she wants to do it with me. She wants to go everywhere and do everything with me so that she can learn and be actively mentored. She doesn't want to wait until she is older to do what God has set before her. So it is with many of her generation. They are looking for those of us who will reach out and grab their hand and pull them into everything we have and know. They want to grab hold of us so that they can grab hold of their future.[1]

NEED TO PREPARE

Deborahs need to prepare. There are young women destined to lead cities, states and nations. There are others called to lead corporations, churches or businesses, or to become judges, doctors, lawyers or leaders. There is a core of healthy radicals who are the movers and shakers of the generation. They will move the world as we know it into a whole new reality. *Who will counsel them on how to move forward and prepare themselves so that they are ready when the opportunity arises?*

When Mordecai asked Esther to plead the cause of the Jews before the king, she replied that any man or woman who approached the king without being summoned would be put to death, unless the king granted an exception. But Mordecai challenged her, telling her that if she were not willing to stand in behalf of the Jewish people, God would raise up another deliverer, adding, "yet who knows whether you have come to the kingdom for such a time as this?" (Esther 4:14).

His words were exactly what Esther needed—the ultimate challenge. She lifted up her voice and said, "I will go to the king, which is against the law; and if I perish, I perish!" (Esther 4:16). She accepted the challenge and stood before the king on behalf of the Jewish nation. She risked her very life to save the Jews, and a whole nation was saved because she was not only wise, but also bold and cunning. My granddaughter's generation is one that will risk their lives, not loving them unto death. The world will have to recognize and embrace them. They will not be denied.

We are in a day when Esthers are arising and will defend Israel. They will defend God's people, whomever and wherever they are, standing boldly before leaders and taking their place as an intercessor and deliverer. They will cry out for those yet held in bondage by a veil of deception, unable to perceive the truth of the gospel. They will travel into nations hostile to the gospel and risk their very lives because of their love for Christ and unbelievers. They are bold enough to believe God for whole nations to disciple.

RISE UP, GRAB HOLD OF THE NEXT GENERATION

I say to my generation of women leaders: Let us rise up and grab the hands of the next generation. Let's become mentors and mothers who will give them everything we have learned over the years. We are pregnant with the birthing of a generation that will arise and change the world. They are our seed whom we must nurture to take our place and go further than we ourselves have been able to go. Let us prepare them to wear the mantles of authority with which God has destined them to be clothed. Let us stand to our feet and cheer them on into the next phase of possessing the gates of the enemy.

I say to the emerging generation: Boldly grab our hands and let us propel you beyond the places we have been able to go. You are coming into your day and your hour. Arise Deborahs, Esthers, Huldahs, Hannahs, Marys, Lydias and Dorcases. You will be mantled with authority and empowered by the apostolic call to overcome every obstacle; taking homes, schools, cities, nations, governments and businesses—wherever God leads you, to invade with boldness. Release His Kingdom everywhere you go with signs, wonders and miracles. You are not ordinary; you are supernatural because of the empowering of His Holy Spirit.

ENDNOTES

Chapter One

1. Chuck D. Pierce and Rebecca Wagner Sytsema, *The Future War of the Church* (Ventura, CA: Renew Books, 2001).
2. Ibid., p. 234.
3. David Yonggi Cho, quoted in Kim Laurence, "Women: Our Most Untapped Resource," *Heartbeat of West Kentucky* 1, no. 1 (July 2000), p. 1.
4. Judy Jacobs, "Warring in the Spirit," *SpiritLed Woman*, October/November 1999, pp. 42-46.
5. Leland Ryken, James C. Wilhoit and Tremper Longman, III, eds., *Dictionary of Biblical Imagery* (Downers Grove, IL: InterVarsity Press, 1998), pp. 64-65.
6. Dr. J. G. Morrison, *Satan's Subtle Attack on Woman* (Kansas City, MO: Nazarene Publishing House, 1996), n.p.

Chapter Two

1. For more on how to break out and break through, see Barbara J. Yoder, *The Breaker Anointing* (Colorado Springs, CO: Wagner Publications, 2001).
2. Bonhoeffer, *The Cost of Discipleship* (London, England: SCM Press, 1959).
3. I consider the New Apostolic Reformation Church to be the modern-day Church of Acts. For further information, see C. Peter Wagner, *Churchquake: The Explosive Power of the New Apostolic Revolution* (Ventura, CA: Regal Books, 2000).

Chapter Three

1. *Biblesoft's New Exhaustive Strong's Numbers and Concordance with Expanded Greek-Hebrew Dictionary* (Seattle, WA: PC Biblesoft and International Bible Translators, Inc., 2003), Greek no. 652.
2. I believe the most recent helpful book on understanding apostolic authority is C. Peter Wagner, *Spheres of Authority* (Wagner Publications: Colorado Springs, CO, 2002).
3. *Biblesoft's New Exhaustive Strong's Numbers and Concordance with Expanded Greek-Hebrew Dictionary*, Greek no. 649.
4. *Merriam-Webster's Dictionary*, 11th edition, s.v. "mandate."
5. Ibid., s.v. "ambassador."
6. I will refer to the Church of Acts as the Apostolic Church.
7. *Biblesoft's New Exhaustive Strong's Numbers and Concordance with Expanded Greek-Hebrew Dictionary*, Greek no. 4641.
8. Though I am speaking to women, women partner with men to accomplish the apostolic mandate. Neither gender will accomplish their task without the other.

9. Several references can be found in Acts. Look at Acts 8:12 and 28:23.

10. *Biblesoft's New Exhaustive Strong's Numbers and Concordance with Expanded Greek-Hebrew Dictionary*, Greek no. 1411.

11. Albert Barnes, *Barnes' Notes* (Seattle, WA: PC Bible Study, Biblesoft, 1998), notes on Romans 16:7.

12. C. F. Keil and Franz Delitzsch, *Keil and Delitzsch Commentary on the Old Testament* (Seattle, WA: PC Bible Study, Biblesoft, 1998), notes on Isaiah 10:27.

13. Ibid.

14. For more information, see Barbara J. Yoder, *The Breaker Anointing* (Colorado Springs, CO: Wagner Publications, 2001), pp 67-68.

Chapter Four

1. Joseph H. Thayer, *The New Thayer's Greek Lexicon of the New Testament* (Peabody, MA: Hendricks Publishers, 1981).

2. Josephus, *Jewish War, IV* (Baltimore, MD: Harvard Clinic Press, 1951).

3. *Merriam-Webster's Dictionary*, s.v. "pioneer."

4. See the New Testament Gospels: Matthew, Mark and Luke.

Chapter Five

1. Betsy Morris, "Trophy Husbands," *Fortune*, October 14, 2002, pp. 78-98.

2. I am not advocating that women leave the home and let their husbands raise their children. This is a decision to be made between a husband and wife. Seed are also children, so we must make sure that our children are given the loving, nurturing and supportive environment to become all they are destined to be. They are our seed, and we must see them through to realizing their potential—the seed that is within them.

3. Patricia Sellers, "True Grit," *Fortune*, October 14, 2002, p. 101.

4. Ibid.

Chapter Six

1. Saira Shah, "Behind the Veil," *Cable News Network (CNN)*, 2001.

Chapter Seven

1. *Merriam-Webster's Dictionary*, 11th edition, s.v. "mantle."

2. *Biblesoft's New Exhaustive Strong's Numbers and Concordance with Expanded Greek-Hebrew Dictionary* (Seattle, WA: PC Biblesoft and International Bible Translators, Inc., 2003), Hebrew no. 155.

3. Ibid., Hebrew no. 3519.

4. Ibid., Hebrew no. 1391 and no. 1380.

5. Ibid., Hebrew no. 117.

6. Ibid., Greek no. 1849.

7. The headquarters of Rhema International is in Rochester, Michigan. Reverend Gruits continues to lead this mission organization.

8. One book I recommend to understand the Ephesians 4:11-12 gifts better

is Richard Eberle, *The Complete Wineskin: Restructuring the Church for the Out Pouring of the Holy Spirit* (Yakima, WA: WinePress Ministries, 1993).

9. C. Peter Wagner, *Humility* (Ventura, CA: Regal Books, 2001).

Chapter Eight

1. Richard LaCayo, "Lifting the Veil," *Time*, December 1, 2001.
2. James Strong, *The New Strong's Exhaustive Concordance of the Bible* (Nashville, TN: Thomas Nelson Publishers, 1984), Hebrew no. 2428.
3. Ibid., Hebrew no. 2342b.
4. Ibid., Hebrew no. 6822. See Ezekiel 3:17; 33:2,6-7.
5. Ibid., Hebrew no. 7950 and no. 7119.

Chapter Nine

1. *Biblesoft's New Exhaustive Strong's Numbers and Concordance with Expanded Greek-Hebrew Dictionary* (Seattle, WA: PC Biblesoft and International Bible Translators, Inc., 2003), Hebrew no. 5782.
2. Ibid., Hebrew no. 5783.
3. I am not saying he was right or wrong; I am using what he did as an example of how an apostle thinks and acts. Study the book of Acts and note the offensive nature of the apostles. They penetrated hostile territories with the gospel.
4. *Biblesoft's New Exhaustive Strong's Numbers and Concordance with Expanded Greek-Hebrew Dictionary,* Greek no. 4752.
5. Ibid., Greek no. 4754.
6. For more information, see Barbara J. Yoder, *The Breaker Anointing* (Colorado Springs, CO: Wagner Publications, 2001). I also strongly recommend two other books: Chuck Pierce and John Dickson, *The Worship Warrior: Ascending in Worship, Descending in War* (Ventura, CA: Regal Books, 2002) and Chuck D. Pierce and Rebecca Wagner Sytsema, *The Future War of the Church* (Ventura, CA: Regal Books. 2001).
7. Patricia C. McKissack and Fredrick McKissack, *Soujourner Truth, Ain't I a Woman?* (New York: F. Watts, 1991).
8. Read C. Peter Wagner, *Spheres of Authority* (Colorado Springs, CO: Wagner Publications, 2002).
9. Bobby Clinton, Class Lecture, Southwestern Christian University Graduate School, September 1997. I suggest every leader should review his books. Two are Dr. J. Robert Clinton, *The Making of a Leader* (Colorado Springs, CO: NavPress, 1988) and *Strategic Concepts* (Altadena, CA: Barnabas Publishers, 1995).

Chapter Ten

1. For more information see Bill Hamon, *Birthing God's Purposes* (Santa Rosa Beach, FL: Christian International Ministries Network, 2000), chapter 10.

RECOMMENDED READINGS

Bushnell, Katherine. *God's Word to Women*. Minneapolis, MN: Christians for Biblical Equality, 2003.

Cunningham, Loren and David Joel Hamilton with Janice Rogers. *Why Not Women?* Seattle, WA: Youth With a Mission Publishing, 2000.

Grady, J. Lee. *Ten Lies the Church Tells Women*. Lake Mary, FL: Charisma House, 2000.

Jacobs, Cindy. *Women of Destiny*. Ventura, CA: Regal Books, 1998.

Jakes, T. D. *Woman Thou Art Loosed*. Shippensburg, PA: Destiny Image Publishing, 1993.

Kroeger, Richard Clark and Catherine Clark Kroeger. *I Suffer Not a Woman*. Grand Rapids, MI: Baker Book House, 1992.

Pierce, Chuck and Rebecca Wagner Systema. *Future War of the Church*. Ventura, CA: Regal Books, 2001.

Pierce, Chuck and John Dickson, *The Worship Warrior*. Ventura, CA: Regal Books, 2002.

Penn-Lewis, Jessie. *The Magna Charta of Woman*. Minneaplis, MN: Bethany Fellowship, Inc., 1975.

Varner, Kelley. *The Three Prejudices*. Shippensburg, PA: Destiny Image Publishing, 1997.

Wagner, C. Peter. *The Spheres of Authority*. Colorado Springs, CO: Wagner Publications, 2002.

Yoder, Barbara J. *The Breaker Anointing*. Colorado Springs, CO: Wagner Publications, 2001.

CONTRIBUTORS

Chuck D. Pierce is vice president of Global Harvest Ministries, president of Glory of Zion International Ministries, national apostle of the U.S. Strategic Prayer Network, and is on the executive board of the International Coalition of Apostles, the Apostolic Council of Prophetic Elders and the International Society of Deliverance Ministers. He has been used by God to intercede and mobilize prayer for local churches, cities and nations. In addition, he coordinates prayer for many of the major spiritual events and gatherings around the world and is a prophet to territories and cities.

Chuck has coauthored several books, including *Prayers That Outwit the Enemy* and *The Future War of the Church,* with Rebecca Wagner Sytsema; *The Worship Warrior,* with John Dickson; and *Restoring Your Shield of Faith,* with Robert Heidler. These and all of Chuck's materials are available through Glory of Zion at 888-965-1099, or by visiting www.glory-of-zion.org.

Apostle **Wanda Joy Studdard** was called into fulltime ministry at Word of Faith Christian Center where she served as associate pastor, staff pastor, minister of music, and special ministry person. In December of 1987, Wanda married Graden Eugene Studdard, Jr. In 1989, they opened Harvest Prayer Center. In September of 1990, Apostle Studdard opened Joy Tabernacle Christian Academy, a school for children in nursery through sixth grade. She began the school with only one student and today it has grown to over 350 students, housing the largest indoor playground in Indianapolis. She is also a playwright who uses drama as a tool for salvation. Apostle Studdard can be seen on Sky Angel Satellite worldwide on her weekly broadcast, *Word Alive Today.*

Apostle Studdard is a woman of God who is hungry for His move and is determined to pay the price to bring that move of God to this generation. She can be contacted at Harvest Prayer Center, 2333 Lafayette Road, Indianapolis, IN 46222; or by calling 317-920-4569. The website address is www.hpcworldwide.com.

Jean Hodges has a national as well as international ministry. Jean believes strongly in team ministry and often travels around the world ministering with her husband, Jim, founder of the Federation of Ministers and Churches, and other apostolic and prophetic teams. She ministers to churches and conferences both in and out of the Federation of Ministers and Churches. Jean has a revelational teaching ministry with an assignment to build the global house of God. Jean's heart is to see people arise and walk in their destiny and inheritance, and her goal is to see God's people rise to the occasion. She releases a strong prophetic anointing for breakthrough. The power of God flows through her for healing deliverance and miracles.

Jean can be contacted at The Federation of Ministers and Churches International, P.O. Box 380894, Duncanville, TX 75138. The website address is www.fmcapostolicnetwork.com.

Jane Hansen serves as president of Aglow International, a worldwide outreach ministry that is impacting the lives of women and their families in more than 151 nations. It is one of the largest international Christian women's organizations in the world, with more than 1,400 groups in the United States and more than 2,100 groups worldwide.

Jane's desire is for God's healing and restoration to reach into women's lives in order that they may embrace all God that wills to do through them in the Body of Christ. An ordained minister, she serves in leadership roles with a number of organizations. She is also the author of *Fashioned for Intimacy: Reconciling Men and*

Women to God's Original Design and *Journey of a Woman* (her autobiography). These and other materials are available through Aglow International, P.O. Box 1749, Edmonds, WA 98020; or by calling 800-793-8126. The website is www.aglow.org.

Barbara J. Yoder is the founder and senior pastor of Shekinah Christian Church, a racially and culturally diverse church in Ann Arbor, Michigan. Barbara is known for her cutting-edge prophetic ministry. She travels extensively within the United States and throughout the world ministering in churches, conferences, and seminars.

Pastor Yoder has a passion to establish the prophetic presence of Jesus as well as see a revival anointing released in cities, regions and nations. She has been instrumental in bringing the prophetic movement together with the prayer movement to pave the way for visitation here and abroad. Recently, she has been teaching and releasing a strong apostolic anointing that will unlock the evangelistic thrust. She is the author of the best-selling book, *The Breaker Anointing,* and is also one of the contributors to the *Women of Destiny Bible,* edited by Cindy Jacobs. These and other materials are available through Shekinah Christian Church (see the contact information page at the end of this book).

CONTACT INFORMATION

Barbara J. Yoder is the apostolic leader of Shekinah
Christian Church. You may contact her through:

Shekinah Christian Church
P.O. Box 2485
Ann Arbor, MI 48103

Office: (734) 662-6040
Fax: (734) 662-5470

www.shekinachurch.org

SCRIPTURE INDEX

SUBJECT INDEX

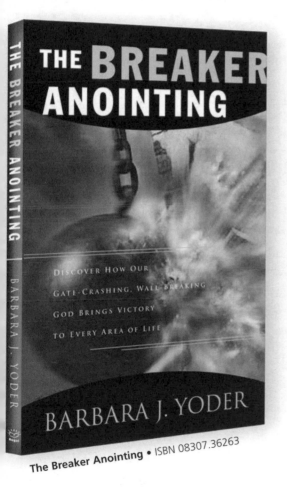

Enrich Your Life

**A Woman's Guide to
Spiritual Warfare**
Quin Sherrer and *Ruthanne Garlock*
ISBN 08307.35186

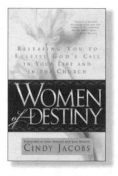

Women of Destiny
Releasing You to Fulfill God's Call
in Your Life and in the Church
Cindy Jacobs
ISBN 08307.18648

**Women: God's
Secret Weapon**
God's Inspiring Message to Women
of Power, Purpose and Destiny
Ed Silvoso
ISBN 08307.28872

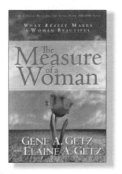

The Measure of a Woman
What Really Makes
a Woman Beautiful
Gene and Elaine Getz
ISBN 08307.32861

**Moments Together
for Couples**
Daily Devotions for Drawing Near
to God and One Another
Dennis and Barbara Rainey
ISBN 08307.17544

**Miracles Happen When
Women Pray**
Eyewitness Stories That Will
Encourage You in Your Prayer Life
Bobbye Byerly
ISBN 08307.26462